PARENTS AT WAR

Custody Battles in Indian Courts

POONAM A BAMBA

Vitasta
LET KNOWLEDGE SPREAD

Published by
Renu Kaul Verma
Vitasta Publishing Pvt Ltd
2/15, Ansari Road, Daryaganj
New Delhi-110 002
info@vitastapublishing.com

ISBN 978-93-86473-99-8

First Edition 2021

MRP ₹495

Edited by Kanagam King
Cover by Somesh Kumar Mishra
Printed by Vikas Computer and Printers

It's dangerous to label and pigeonhole children

I am the child.
All the world waits for my coming,
All the earth watches with interest
To see what I shall become.
Civilisation hangs in the balance,
For what I am, the world of tomorrow will be.

I am the child.
I have come into your world
About which I know nothing.
Why I came I know not.
How I came I know not.
I am curious, I am interested.

I am the child.
You hold in your hand my destiny,
You determine largely,
Whether I shall succeed or fail.
Give me, I pray you,
Those things that make for happiness.
Train me, I beg you,
That I may be a blessing to the world.

-Mamie Gene Cole

Contents

Acknowledgements

This book would not have come into existence, had I not been recording my experiences in court, in my daily journal, a habit which is a gift from my father. I am deeply indebted to my father, Dr Janak Raj Jai, who has been a great inspiration.

I am indebted to Ms Sujata Madhok for painstakingly tidying up the manuscript and for her invaluable inputs.

I am also thankful to Man Mohanji for his suggestion to explain the legal process one needs to follow for obtaining child custody. It has been immensely useful.

I also record my gratitude to the editor Kanagam King for fine-tuning the manuscript.

I am indebted to my husband Anil, my sons Apoorv and Ishaan, my daughter-in-law Vidushi, and my grandson Meir for sparing me for this work.

I am grateful to Ishita Pandey for her sensitive poetry compositions, which I have used in this manuscript.

I would like to thank Young Myra, Nitya, and the other children who contributed the lovely pictures that have been included in the manuscript.

I acknowledge the contribution of litigating parents, their children, and other family members who presented varied life situations before me, which set me thinking, and led to the book you have in your hands.

Support of Jyoti, the caretaker of my home, cannot go unacknowledged. Without her help, it would not have been possible for me to spare any time in pursuing my passion.

My heartfelt gratitude to each and every one who, in any manner, has been associated with me in bringing this work to its fruition.

Preface

In my decade-and-a-half long career as a Judge, I have found custody litigation to be the most painful litigation not only for children and parents but also for judges. The increase in break-up of families and the rising divorce rate has many types of fallout. Children of divorced couples are the ones who really bear the brunt. The parents may move on with their lives but children carry the trauma for a lifetime. It is the children, who get manipulated and torn apart emotionally during the process of separation, divorce, and custody. When the parents separate, the immediate question that arises is—who shall have the custody of the child? Courts are also faced with the predicament of how to ensure the access of the non-custodial parent; and how to make both parents aware of their responsibility for the protection, safety, health, education, and general well-being of the child.

Behind the dusty files, I met so many children whose lives had been tossed and turned because of the turbulent relationship between their parents. These files threw up poignant tales of despair and trauma faced by children of broken or breaking marriages, which I privately poured into my daily journal. This book is an attempt to present to parents, their families, and their advocates, the stories of these unhappy children, so that they put first, the interests of the little angels whose custody they seek so determinedly and often aggressively.

Bringing this book to a conclusion was quite a task. When I told my dear friend, Maninder, that this was giving me stress she asked, 'Why do you want to write the book?' That set me thinking. A few days ago while I was fine-tuning my draft, the answer presented itself to me. I realised that I feel connected to myself, when I write. I find myself in my writings.

May I call it serendipity, that *Impersonal Life*, a book by Joseph S Benner written in 1914, came my way at this juncture. Benner says that all writings are channelled/impersonal. Though he made this comment in the context of spiritual writing, it further clarified my 'need' to write. Maybe, I am the chosen one to share the stories of pain and trauma of little children.

I also came across another perspective on such writing. I read that such writing is not *lekhan* (writing), but *abhivyakti* (expression). Perhaps expression of one's own self.

I thus allowed myself to be used for sharing these stories in the hope that parents may get a glimpse of what they make children undergo in their zeal to win their custody.

Now, a little bit about the nature of cases that are filed for child custody and the varied reasons for these. May I say that, like drugs, custody litigation can also be spurious. Such cases may seem genuine at first glance but all are not so. Though I have not carried out any empirical study, it will not be incorrect to say that roughly 40 to 50 per cent of custody litigation has actually nothing to do with the custody of the child. The custody petition is only a facade to pursue a hidden agenda, which could range from avenging the divorce petition filed by the custodial parent (a parent in custody of the child) to a counter blast to a dowry case, to a complaint by the wife under the Domestic Violence Act. It could even be to pressurise or harass the wife who has filed a petition for maintenance for herself and the child. In such cases, the husband's petition would generally suggest that the custody of the child be given to him if the wife is unable to maintain the child.

Every story, I found, was layered. Moving slowly through each case helped me burrow through various layers and discover the real story behind the story put up before the court. Each day in court threw at me a new challenge. Every custody case was distinct from the other. Even in the same category of cases, there was nothing repetitive. Each story carried a different emotion. Some were plain and simple angry stories; some, very dejected; some hurtful; and some revengeful. At the bottom of most of these stories, all I found was insecurity. Custodial parents are insecure because they fear losing control. Non-custodial parents' battles generally arise from a place of want, a feeling of deprivation.

One of the categories of such custody petitions is petitions filed by grandparents after the death of the child's father. This kind of litigation generally emanates from the apprehension that their daughter-in-law (child's mother) may ask for the child's share in the joint family property. To insulate themselves from any claim by the child (through the mother) to the father's/ancestral property in future, the paternal grandparents demand custody of the child. These are generally the cases where the mother shifts to her parental house along with the child after the death of her husband. There are also situations where the child's mother remarries. The moment that happens, the paternal grandparents get another weapon in their arsenal. They generally allege that the child will not be taken care of by the new family or that the mother has left the child with her parents, who are incapable of bringing up the child. They suddenly remember that the child is the only *nishaani* (only living symbol) of their son, the only torchbearer of their lineage. Here the claim is not as much to genuinely have the custody of the grandchild as it is to protect themselves from any future property claim. This kind of hidden agenda of the grandparents is generally revealed on a little probing during counselling, while making efforts to bring about an amicable settlement. Generally, within no time, such petitions are withdrawn through a settlement laying down that the child's mother shall not stake any claim in the family property for herself or for the child. Such settlements are oblivious to the fact that nobody can contract out the child's rights, not even the child's own mother.

There is yet another category of child custody claims. Sometimes, when the child's mother dies under suspicious circumstances, the child's father and paternal grandparents are accused of death by harassment. The maternal grandparents usually take away the child and the father files a petition seeking custody of his own child. Such claims may or may not be genuine; the custody petition may have been filed only to pressurise the wife's parents to tone down their allegations in criminal cases related to the wife's death.

Such fake custody litigation, where the true intent is to achieve an oblique purpose, is wasteful and burdens the already burdened justice system. It is also physically, mentally, and financially taxing to the other side. And of course, such litigation also puts the child under stress.

Genuine custody claims are painful and traumatic for all concerned. They really tax the judges, mentally and emotionally. It is deeply traumatic to see the child being pulled in opposite directions by parents 'genuinely' (that is how they perceive themselves to be) wanting to provide the best upbringing to the child. However, both, unknowingly, cause permanent damage to the psyche of the child. Such custody battles may lead to children suffering from personality disorders.

Having dealt with family litigation for about seven years, the fact that dysfunctional families cause immense trauma to children was not new to me. But dealing with individual cases for child custody brought me face to face with the tug of war between the spouses for custody; the insecurity of the custodial parent apprehending loss of custody, and the non-custodial parent's fear of losing the affection of the child. I saw close up the trauma of warring parents and the sandwiched children. I also realised what a huge impact such conflicts leave on the character and personality of the children.

It was painful to see such children develop the art of manipulating the parents to protect themselves. I noticed that with the passage of time such children unfortunately learnt to extract a pound of flesh from both parents. It was grotesque to see such children deriving pleasure from causing pain to parents desperately wanting to spend time with them. The way they bargained with the parents left me dumbstruck on many an occasion. Some children even played 'double agents' and it was appalling to see the parents play into their hands.

The extent to which such a tug of war for custody impacted the young minds, scarring their character forever, really saddened me and made me reflect deeply.

Heartfelt conversations with some children revealed that some of these children were 'runaway' children, living with a parent but with a total disconnect. Some of them had created a world of their own and put up a virtual screen to protect themselves from the world in which they felt unloved. Sometimes they perceived themselves to be the cause of discord between their parents. In the virtual world, they found an outlet for their emotions and also looked for parent figures.

Another revelation that emerged was that because of their lopsided personalities, some children had no close friends, as they were not able to trust easily. As a result, they were happier with their virtual friends on social media. Such children tend to lose touch with real human beings—adding further to their personality issues.

This reminds me of the movie *Happy End,* which depicts a child who runs away from life into the virtual world of the mobile and the computer screen. Social media becomes a surrogate social circle for the child.

Sometimes I found it to be a herculean task to talk to the real person while interacting with such children during counselling. It was painful to see how these children enveloped themselves with layer after layer of acquired social behaviour to protect their own beings. They used this to protect themselves from the incessant assault on their personalities, unknowingly heaped by both the parents, while extracting information about the other parent or by constantly seeking the child's approval, to meet their own insecurities. Such children adopted dishonest ways to please both the parents.

Communicating with these children was a very demanding exercise. Only gradual interaction over numerous sittings helped me lift the veil off the facade that they had so painstakingly built around their inner world. This not only taught me patience but also helped me develop a technique of when to engage and when to immediately drop a conversation. The child's facial expression and body language generally enabled me to take a call.

It was quite interesting to see that such children would agree to share their feelings—towards their parents, and their preferences of staying with one or the other—only after extracting a promise from me that I would not share it with their parents. The extent of pressure they felt was revealed when some children would want me to ensure that the door of the chamber was tightly closed and there was no one around, before they opened up. Such precautions were not foolproof. On a number of occasions, I saw children being subjected to a volley of questions by the custodial parent as soon as they stepped out of my chamber or the court premises. One mother was seen shaking and threatening her son as she could guess that he had agreed to spend half of his holidays with his father.

I felt that such parents themselves need counselling to make them aware of the extent of trauma they inflict on children by their behaviour.

This book is an endeavour to share stories of such children and parents with a sincere hope that it is able to mirror the concerns of all the stakeholders—custodial and non-custodial parents, the society, and most of all, the children of broken homes.

I am reminded of the words of the Nobel laureate Kailash Satyarthi of *Bachpan Bachao Andolan* fame that you may address the children's problems and provide for their future but you can never restore their childhood. Once lost, it is lost forever.

That is the kind of responsibility with which we need to deal with our children. Writing about the repetitive script(s) which unfolded before me has not been easy because at times I felt that people may already know what I am about to share. But I was motivated by an inner calling to share such stories, as I felt that people don't see in themselves what others can see in them and how it harms vulnerable lives. I put my pen to paper with the intent of sharing some of the stories to show how certain behaviours affect innocent lives, and the book you are holding in your hand today just spread onto the paper.

Every story in this book is inspired by true events and cases. The characters however, have been camouflaged and the stories a bit fictionalised to avoid resemblance with the true characters.

This book is an effort to share real-life stories to bring parents face to face with the children's reality.

Happy and thoughtful reading!

FROM MY DIARY

Hemant realised his love needed no words as he sat quietly with an arm around Kush.

New Beginnings

'Hey there! Are you alright?'
Asked his soul peeking from inside.
Closing his eyes, he gave a dainty smile.
That kid of nine has seen it for a while.
Sitting by the desk, he asked his soul,
'I have everything I need, I want no more.
But there's something I'm missing, can you help me find?'
'Father's shoulders,' the soul replied.
Those days are gone when his hands were held high –
One from the left and one from the right –
Custody battle, his mom is the winner.
In a life without father, he is only a beginner.

—Ishita Pandey (Seventeen years old)

HEMANT LAY SPRAWLED on the silvery sands of an isolated beach in South Goa. Nearby, his son Kush was happily throwing into the sea, the seashells he had collected painstakingly, one by one. Kush would wait for the waves to rise before he threw each shell, so he could see it dance up and down.

Hemant and Kush were just a foot apart from each other. One lying with his back on the grainy sand and the other lost in gazing at the sea. Looking at the happy portrait of father and son, it was hard to believe that it had taken four years of intense counselling and eventually a court order to bring them together.

Grains of sand shone silver on Hemant's back intermittently whenever the sun managed to push the clouds away. Hemant had chosen to spend the morning by the sea with Kush to share some quality time with him.

Kush could not spurn his father's entreaties to get up a little early to 'enjoy' the sea. Had it been Neera, his mother, Kush would have turned to the other side and covered his ears with his pillow. But, he did not want to hurt Hemant who had fought so long for this holiday with him.

Neera had left home four years ago with Kush, who was barely two years old then. She had insulated Kush—from what she perceived as Hemant's 'bad influence'—for all those years. The natural connection between father and son had been lost over the last four years.

As Hemant lay on the sand, he seemed to have slipped into a trance while the sun pushed the clouds away. He was unaffected by the harsh sun now hitting his body hard. Kush hopped from one activity to the other.

Hemant was jolted out of his trance by Kush's squeal 'Papa...See that animal!' His lips gently stretched into a smile as he tilted his head to see Kush excitedly watching a snail moving at its own pace, with its neck craned out of the shell.

Something moved inside Hemant by the pleasant resonance of the word 'Papa', which he had not heard for so long.

On sensing some danger, the snail retracted into its shell while Kush came running and crashed into Hemant giving him a giant hug. It took only a split second for that old bond between Hemant and Kush to revive. In that embrace, both melted into each other.

The sound of the high tide waves hitting the sea sounded like hundreds of conches blowing together. The spray fell softly on Hemant and Kush, as if the very heavens were celebrating the moment.

That embrace relieved Hemant of the anxiety he had been nursing on how to connect with Kush. He relaxed, realising he did not need to verbalise the script he had been practising mentally for the last seven days to be able to talk to Kush. He had spent hours debating whether to call him Kush beta or Kush darling, and plotting out various schemes to break the ice, like taking him to a restaurant of his choice or perhaps to a toy store…

Hemant needed none of this, as they sat quietly, with an arm around each other. Words were no longer needed to communicate. Life is so simple and beautiful without language. They exchanged so much in those five minutes.

It took Hemant no time to bond with his own blood, but he had to plead hard before the court to procure interim custody of his son. Hemant had to use every word in his dictionary and to raise every emotional plea in his kitty, including shedding tears to convince the court about the genuineness of his love and longing to spend some time with his child. But, at this moment he needed no arguments. Tears trickled down his cheeks onto his bare chest as he embraced Kush. He felt the cloud of sadness lifting off his heart.

They walked back to the hotel room in a happy silence. Kush kept swinging their hands with their fingers intertwined like a creeper tightly clinging to the wall. They did not bother to shake the sand off their feet before entering the plush room of the five-star hotel where they were put up.

In the room, they looked at each other and exchanged a smile. Kush was hot and rushed off to have a bath.

Hemant was still lost in his thoughts when he heard Kush calling him from the bathroom.

'Yes…coming, dear,' shouted Hemant, loudly enough to be audible to Kush who was singing and dancing under the shower.

The Family Court, being the *parens patriae*[1] is under bounden duty to assess the welfare of the child before any custody order is made. It is not the interest of either parent that matters. The guiding star is the *welfare of the child*, which is of paramount consideration. The court has to discharge its *parens patriae* obligations transcending the jurisdiction created by law for administration purposes.

Could the court have imagined that love could sprout between Hemant and Kush during their togetherness at Goa, I had wondered. More so, in the light of Neera's extreme resistance to the proposal and Kush's own reservations about spending time with his father in Goa.

'Kush has not stayed overnight with Hemant for the last four years; he has hardly met Hemant during this long period.

1 In law, it refers to the public policy power of the state/court to intervene against an abusive or negligent parent, legal guardian, or informal caretaker, and to act as the parent of any child or individual who is in need of protection

How can his custody be handed over to Hemant for a full week?' Neera had fiercely argued, leaving her advocate—who had not been allowed to speak a word—red-faced.

'Wouldn't you like to give the child a chance to bond with his father?' I had politely asked Neera.

How do you expect the child to be comfortable in his father's company—when he hardly shares any togetherness?' Neera argued.

'Don't you think it will only traumatise the child to force him to spend such a long time span with his father, who has never bothered to interact with him?' she added.

Neera's words incited Hemant, silent until then, to retaliate. 'Please mind your statement,' he said sharply.

I had quite expected this reaction because of the way Neera had gestured towards Hemant to portray him as an absolutely uncaring father.

'Ma'am, you ask her, who is responsible for my non-interaction,' Hemant turned to me with pleading eyes before continuing.

'She has been blocking all my efforts to get in touch with Kush. Whenever I call, she cooks up one excuse or the other to scuttle my efforts to be in touch with Kush,' he said.

'When I call in the afternoon, I am told to call the next evening as Kush is sleeping; and in the evening he has to go to a friend's birthday party and will not be able to talk to me. She has thousands of excuses to keep me away from Kush.'

'She even turned down my request to buy a mobile phone for Kush so I could talk to him or he could call me up,' fumed Hemant.

'Neera does not even let me visit Kush at his school,'

complained Hemant. You tell me, ma'am, what should I do?' he asked me.

His desperation to meet his son was evident.

Counselling Neera did not yield any solution. Apprising her that spending time with both the parents is essential for the child's holistic growth and that her rigid stand only deprived Kush of his father's love and affection, had no visible impact on Neera.

'I can't send Kush to spend an entire week with Hemant. ...No way ma'am,' she said emphatically.

'Who is she to decide, ma'am? Have I no right over my child?' asked Hemant. 'I am the child's father and have equal rights over my child,' he concluded.

'Where were you when Kush was unwell?' Neera pressed the gun even before Hemant said his last word.

'Ask your own selfish self,' retorted Hemant.

'Did you ever inform me about his health? Rather, you have never let me come near my own child. Did you alone produce the child, you bloody...?' Hemant stopped in the nick of time, relieving me of the task of delivering a scolding.

Neera was holding herself back, I could see from the corner of my eyes, but she would not have hesitated to bare her knuckles, had Hemant ventured to continue with his tirade. She did issue a thinly veiled threat. To my good fortune, the advocates from both the sides were mature and intervened to pacify their respective clients.

Hemant, Neera, and their advocates talked only about the rights of the parents over the child.

Is anyone thinking about Kush, I wondered.

The lawyers started quoting law in their favour. Neera's

lawyer made me read judgment after judgment of the higher courts to demonstrate that it would not be in Kush's welfare to hand over his interim custody to Hemant. However, the advocate offered to make an effort to persuade Neera to agree to hand over Kush's custody for at least a night. Neera immediately rejected this, leaving her lady advocate a little hurt.

The polite advocate, shaking off the hurt at her proposal being rejected, made another attempt to make Neera see reason. She whispered something in Neera's ear to convince her to agree but soon gave up, lest she lose her client. From Neera's intemperate behaviour, and how her body was now shaking with anger, it was clear that she felt threatened by the thought of losing sole control over Kush. Kush had become the only reference point in her life and if that were lost, she would be finished, I could see.

Parents unwittingly start believing that they own their children like any other property, and any perceived interference in that ownership destabilises their life! Differences between spouses are projected onto the child. Any hurt caused to a spouse is made the ground to assert that the other is not worthy of interacting with the child, as in the present case.

Recently, a judge dealing with custody rights in the divorce case filed by Angelina Jolie against Brad Pitt, asked Angelina to ensure that their kids' relationship with their father was not disturbed. A leading daily reported that the concerned judge while observing that it was critical for the children to have a healthy and strong relationship with their parents, ordered Angelina to give the cell phone numbers of their six children to Brad so that he could call them whenever he wanted. The judge also made it clear that in case Brad Pitt was not allowed to interact with the children, the court could order reduction in the time the children spent with Angelina or even order primary physical custody to Brad Pitt.

One may not have proved to be a good husband or wife. However, that alone cannot brand him/her as a bad father/mother. One may not be a good husband but may be a great father.

I so much wanted to tell Neera not to use Kush as a weapon to fight her own battle with Hemant but stopped short of doing that. At that time, in the state of mind she was, I was sure Neera would not have been open to any advice.

My failure to persuade them to arrive at a consensus compelled me to speak with them privately in my chamber, where it is easier for the spouses to reconsider their decision, than in the open court, where any change in the stand taken is considered a weakness.

I counselled both Neera and Hemant in the chamber separately as well as together. But to no avail. This was a last-ditch attempt to bring about a consensus on sharing Kush's custody during his vacations.

Having met with no success with his parents, I had an interaction with Kush in the chamber. It took me quite an effort to make him comfortable and to assure him that he could trust me. I removed my black coat and neckband and shared the sofa with Kush. Our conversation however did not move beyond the exchange of niceties, getting to know his name, the class he studied in, his favourite subject and teacher, and so on.

It takes time to build trust for children to confide in you. Sometimes, a child may not have the vocabulary to articulate his feelings and choices.

The palm tree Kush drew, possibly inspired by the tree outside the chamber window.

Kush drew a tall palm tree on the A-four size paper I handed over to him while I pretended to be busy with some reading material, in the hope that his drawing may give me some clue about his feelings.

Trees represent our egos and ambitions, I had read in an article authored by a leading child psychologist.

Child psychologists say that children's drawings provide a window to their inner world. They are the actual representation of their thoughts and feelings; they speak volumes about their psyche. But hasty conclusions on the basis of one sketch were surely avoidable. Kush was possibly inspired by the tree outside the window of my chamber.

To draw a meaningful conclusion, one has to compare a child's drawings over a reasonable period of time. It is also important to pay attention to colours used by a child. For family court judges, time is a rare commodity in view of the pendency of a large number of cases crying for their attention, so they hardly get to interact with children for a long time span. But there have been cases where a few sketches provided clues on what was going on inside the child's mind.

Here, I am reminded of Kavya, whose physical custody was with her mother. She emphatically declined her father's request to accompany him to Orissa during her summer vacations to spend time with cousins and grandparents. Her drawings depicted all the things she hated about Orissa. She was negative about everything to do with her father.

Children, who are not tutored, are more likely to pour out their true thoughts and feelings onto the canvas. There are, however, kids who are so thoroughly tutored by the custodial parent over a long period of time that their views about the other parent are absolutely coloured.

I did not want to push Kush too far lest he raise his guard to ward off any perceived intrusion from my side. We just shook hands before I said bye to him while extracting a promise that he would come to see me again soon. I was reminded of a beautiful story about a fox and a little prince shared by Saraswathi Vasudevan, a yoga therapist/trainer, in *Life Positive*, a monthly magazine, while talking about how to befriend our breath. It read:

> 'One can only understand the things one tames,' the Fox tells the Little Prince. 'If you want a friend, tame me...You must be very patient. First, you will sit down at a little distance from me–like that–in the grass. I shall watch you out of the corner of my eye, and you will say nothing. But every day, you can sit a little closer to me...'
>
> —The Little Prince
> by Antoine de Saint –Exupery

The fox in the story presents a very important pre-condition for developing a friendship; the time you invest and the loving attention you give, she explained. Saraswathi emphasised that this is the kind of relationship one seeks to establish with one's own breath through practices such as *pranayama* (the practice of breath control in Yoga).

The moment I read this, I realised that this is also a technique to establish a rapport with children.

As the interim custody application for Kush was filed just a week before the courts were to close down for summer vacations, there was immense pressure on me to pass the custody order while striking a delicate balance between the child's welfare and a father's longing to be with his own son.

The next time when Kush met me in the chamber, he seemed more at ease and took the liberty to walk around, inspecting every nook and corner, before he settled down on the sofa near the window.

'This is such a nice window to look out from,' he said excitedly while sniffing the air.

'Which tree is this, Aunty?' he suddenly asked. I tried hard to recollect the name of the tree. I must answer this, in order to win his confidence, I thought.

'It is a *Kadamb* tree,' I told Kush with confidence. 'This is the same tree under which Lord Krishna used to play the flute,' I added. Seeing Kush watch a pair of birds hiding in the thick foliage of the Kadamb tree, I asked him, 'Do you know the name of these birds?'

'Oh! These are the same birds, which visit our backyard...I have also seen them in my school park,' answered Kush.

'But you haven't told me their names.'

'Hmmmm...,' he tapped his forehead with his small forefinger but without any success.

'Do you give up? Shall I tell you the name?' I asked him.

Kush assessed the expression on my face and my body language. Feeling assured that I was not putting him down, he said, 'Yessss...tell me the name.'

'These are common *mynahs,*' I told him. He nodded in affirmation.

The tree and those mynahs helped me break the ice. Kush was now comfortable with me. But he became quiet the moment I veered the conversation towards the idea that he spend a week with his father. He immediately pointed towards a parakeet, which had joined the mynahs on the Kadamb tree.

Kush pointed towards a parakeet, which had joined the mynahs on the Kadamb tree.

I left it at that, hoping for a breakthrough the next time. He left with a smile on his face.

The skill of the Judge lies in ascertaining what would be in the best interest of the child. This skill cannot be acquired by reading books or listening to experts on the subject. It calls for something more than the law—knowledge of human behaviour, and experience gained on the job, which is, to connect to one's own self, to be able to access one's intuitive power—what people generally call *sixth sense.* Knowledge is only one of the tools. The essence of this jurisdiction as *parens patriae* lies in how we use knowledge plus intuition. A Family

Court Judge needs to quickly assimilate the peculiar facts and circumstances of each case, past experiences with spouses in similar situations, the child's reaction, and his/her own gut feeling, to find a solution suitable to all the stakeholders, and which serves the best interest of the child. In the first few meetings with the child and the parents, one may not be able to arrive at a solution.

The Judge is supposed to work out a solution, in the most hopeless of situations. Involvement of parents in finding a solution pays in the long run as it is their own solution. Consensus is rare to find but the options thrown up by the parents help in finding the middle path.

However, I was not so fortunate in Kush's case. I had yet another interaction with Kush, the day after. 'Good morning, aunty,' Kush wished me jauntily as soon as he entered the chamber.

'Would you like to draw something while I finish an assignment?' I asked Kush.

'No.' Kush seemed much more confident and at ease than ever before. From his body language, I could sense that he was ready to have the conversation about spending time with his father.

'Where will he take me?' asked Kush.

'How do you like Goa?' I asked.

'Oh, I love beaches.'

'Your Papa wants to take you to Goa for a week,' I informed him.

'Can we go just for two days,' asked Kush, after a long pause.

'Would that not be too short a period for such a long journey?' I asked.

'It just takes about two hours from Delhi to reach Goa by air aunty. It's not that long a journey,' he answered wisely.

Kush's predicament was written all over his face. This was not strange to me, as I have seen children undergo immense stress in their efforts not to displease the custodial parent while also trying to make the other parent happy. It is painful to see children struggle to hide their desire to spend lavish holidays with the non-custodial parent.

I allowed one week's interim custody of Kush to Hemant.

The moment the order was pronounced, Neera almost screamed, as if she had been sure that Hemant's request for interim custody would be turned down. 'I will challenge this order in the High Court,' she threatened while alleging that the Court had not considered with seriousness the less than desirable conduct of Hemant towards Kush. Suddenly, Neera started rummaging through her huge fuchsia pink bag, searching for something. That huge bag in the crook of her arm could have stored a month's grocery. It seemed as if she carried all her woes in that Versace bag.

Luckily, she found what she was frantically searching for. When she put that white and blue nebuliser near her nostrils, I realised that she desperately needed to breathe. A scare ran through my being, imagining the worst—had she not been able to find her nebuliser.

Neera, I realised, felt choked, as she remained stuck in her own viewpoint, not ready to understand that allowing the child to spend time with the father would bring happiness to Kush and also strengthen her own bond with him. Letting go of her rigidity would bring peace and happiness to all of them. She seemed hell bent on romancing her misery.

I left it to the cosmos to take charge, which had brought the parents and the child before me.

Neera's reaction was proof of how parents make the custody of the child a question of their own life and death, as if their existence solely depends upon the child. Parents unknowingly start measuring their importance by the child's denial of the non-custodial parent. I felt it was important for Neera to understand that Kush's willingness to spend time with his father was not a rejection of her. Parental pressure seriously undermines the childhood of the children. It is a kind of command that if you wish to belong to me, then you necessarily have to disregard the other (parent).

The passing of an interim custody order involves so much of weighing and balancing, to ensure that the child's interest is not harmed in any manner. As per law[2], the wish of a child of the age of Kush, who is capable of expressing feelings, is a vital consideration while deciding custody. Such a wish must be given effect to for the overall satisfaction of the child and healthy growth of his mind and body.

The fact that my decision worked well in Kush's case gave me immense satisfaction. The sparkle brought about by the togetherness of father and son could not have been imagined and cannot be described in a legal order. Neera, of course, did not appreciate the love flowing between Kush and Hemant. Her deep fixation with her own hurt did not allow her to see anything beyond that. She fortified her existence and identity with the proud 'possession' of the child.

I sincerely feel that such couples really need constant counselling. I wish Neera could confine her conflict with

---

2 Sub Section (3) of Section 17 of The Guardians and Wards Act, 1890

Hemant to him only and not use Kush as a pawn to pursue her agenda against her husband.

I have experienced that parents refuse to understand that they do not own their children and cannot deal with them as if they were inanimate objects. Parents do no good by loading impressionable children with their own beliefs about people.

- As per law, the wishes of a child grown up enough to make an intelligent choice have to be considered/respected while allowing/disallowing interim/permanent custody.
- Parents need to trust the process because, while deciding the custody issue, besides assessing the welfare of the child, a Family Court has the delicate task of dealing with the differences between the spouses and their accusations against each other.
- A spouse's own hurt at the hands of the other, should not be made a reason for depriving a child of the love and warmth of the other parent.
- Parental pressure seriously undermines children's healthy growth. Ill behaviour of either of the parents towards the other or towards the child can scar the child for a lifetime.
- Parents should check whether they are operating from an exaggerated sense of victimhood.
- Measuring one's own worth by a child's rejection of the other parent is a perfect recipe for disaster.
- A parent does not own a child. Children only come into this world through two human beings. They do not belong to them.
- Parents need to appreciate and respect the child's needs and choices.

Ram Prasad's dark face would be distorted while demeaning his wife.

Scarred Forever

'IF HE HAS issues with me, he should deal with me. Why did he do this to my son?' screamed Neela and burst into tears.

'He has scarred the child for life,' she said in between sobs. Such a sharp reaction from Neela was quite expected, given the extreme measure her husband had resorted to.

The custody of their only child, their seven-year-old son Minku, was with the mother, Neela. Minku's father, Ram Prasad, who was always accompanied by his sister on every date of hearing, would invariably start his submissions by cribbing that his wife simply keeps fleecing him of money but does not allow him the custody of the child. His common refrain was that he was being used as an ATM for drawing money every month but he did not get to interact with the child. His monotonous rhetoric would tire my ears. His dark face would be distorted while demeaning his wife. He would use all possible adjectives for her, calling her greedy, saying she was using the child to extract money, and terming her family a bunch of beggars. His hatred spilt out as he called his in-laws all sorts of names.

I thought of putting some sense into that dull-head. Perhaps I had underestimated his capacity. Asking him to behave was like touching a hornet's nest. Seeing his uncalled for outburst and sensing that things had started spiralling out of control, I thought of counselling both in my chamber and asked them to wait.

I spoke to Neela in the chamber, after duly explaining the process of reconciliation/chamber counselling, and seeking Ram Prasad's permission to talk to her first. But he still kept peeping into my chamber, time and again, like an irrepressible jack-in-the-box, as if to say, 'don't forget to call me to hear my story.' I was compelled to be curt with him.

Neela explained that there was no possibility of their living together. She also made it clear that she would not part with the custody of Minku even for a day, pleading that Ram Prasad was emotionally unstable. She claimed that he was under the influence of his sister, who had instigated him to claim custody, although, he could not take care of the child because of his long working hours. To my relief, she finally agreed to Ram Prasad meeting the child for three to four hours but in the presence of a counsellor.

Chamber counselling with Ram Prasad hardly helped in breaking the impasse. He insisted upon having weekend custody of Minku.

Left with no option, I started the custody hearing in the court. Neela had not even finished narrating her apprehension of their son being unsafe in the father's custody, when Ram Prasad rolled up the sleeves of his dark brown Nehru-collared *kurta* and said she was lying. He began to shout that he was being mala fide deprived of his child's custody.

Sometimes I do allow spouses to enact their drama and vent out their emotions. But Ram Prasad was now exceeding all limits of decency. I gestured towards his lawyer to take charge. But his decent lawyer could hardly control his client.

Suddenly, Neela walked up to Ram Prasad and slapped him, catching all of us unaware. There was pin-drop silence, the very next moment.

Ram Prasad was at a loss of words, perhaps he was still assimilating the enormity of that slap. Neela began apologising, trying to explain that she lost control when he maligned her parents by alleging that the maintenance he paid for the child was being used by them. Apologies from both sides saved the day. The hearing was adjourned for another day.

Ram Prasad's petition for custody talked more about his differences with Neela and her parents than about his suitability to be appointed as guardian of his son. The list of woes, narrated in great detail, started from day one of his marriage to Neela. He had mentioned how he and his family were cheated by Neela's family by giving low-quality furniture and cheap clothing in dowry; how they were insulted by serving sub-standard food to the guests; how the *baraat* (the groom's wedding procession in North India) was not welcomed properly and were not taken care of; how arrangements for the guests' overnight stay were not proper, etc.

Ram Prasad had not left any stone unturned in portraying Neela in a poor light by narrating her (perceived) bad behaviour. He said she did not touch Ram Prasad's parents' feet on getting up in the morning; she dressed inappropriately; she ate breakfast even before his parents had eaten; she talked to her parents and family members over the phone almost every day, and so on and so forth. How were all these facts material in determining the issue of guardianship and the child's custody, was anybody's guess. The only assertions relevant to the prayer for custody were about his financial soundness and that the child would be looked after by his sister and parents.

Family courts deal with strange differences between spouses and their family members, exotic accusations against each other and each other's families, half-baked truths, facts and perceptions blown out of proportion, and an exaggerated sense of victimhood. The judge has to assimilate the peculiarity of each situation at a lightning speed before things get out of control.

During the chamber meeting with Minku, it was apparent that he had drifted away from his father. Keeping in mind Ram Prasad's mercurial temper and volatile temperament, he was granted visitation rights for about four hours, once in a fortnight, at a public place. It was decided that the meeting would take place in the presence of a counsellor, allowing Neela's request, as her apprehensions could not be brushed aside lightly, considering the peculiarity of the situation.

With small hiccups, initially this arrangement went on well. After about two months, Ram Prasad prayed that he be allowed to take the child to a public park to play cricket. Neela agreed to this, assured by the presence of the counsellor.

On the fateful day, the counsellor picked up the child from Neela's place and met Ram Prasad near the park.

Ram Prasad said he had forgotten the bat and tricked the counsellor into going to his residence for it. On reaching his house, Ram Prasad asked the counsellor to wait in the lobby area while he went inside to 'fetch the bat'. Meanwhile, his sister served buttermilk to the counsellor, insisting that he have it, as it was hot outside. After drinking the buttermilk, the counsellor felt an uneasy churning in his stomach and was guided to the toilet by a servant. When he stepped into the toilet, it was locked from outside. No amount of banging helped.

Someone opened the door after fifteen-twenty minutes. He was already feeling weak due to loose motions and the child was not to be seen.

But his trauma was not yet over. Ram Prasad's sister asked him to rest in a room, saying the child was waiting there. The moment the counsellor stepped into the room, she threw chilly powder on his face and locked the room from outside. The saving grace was that the counsellor was carrying his mobile phone. He dialled 100 and was rescued by the police. But, by that time, Ram Prasad had vanished with his son, along with his sister.

The counsellor's complaint put the criminal justice system into motion.

The episode left me with immense anxiety for the well-being of the child. I dissected in my mind every step I took to reach the decision of allowing Ram Prasad to play with his son in a park. Had I done the right thing by allowing this indulgence to Ram Prasad? I wondered.

Neela's lustreless face at the hearing immediately after the kidnapping travelled home with me. I could not breathe easy till the child was traced to a remote village in Madhya Pradesh at Ram Prasad's distant relative's place.

Was Ram Prasad's act pardonable?

Knowing the complexities of the human mind, it was not so easy to deconstruct Ram Prasad's act. From his outbursts on the previous hearing, I could only make out that his action was driven by his feeling of entitlement and orchestrated by emotional instability. He had always been saying that he was not getting custody although he was paying maintenance for the child. I think that it was his way of ensuring that he got value for his money.

I wish he could understand the enormity of his deed. He was oblivious to the lifelong trauma he had caused his son at an impressionable age. All this only to have the value for the money he had been paying for the boy's maintenance. Ram Prasad did not care a hoot about the wishes of his child. He simply wanted to possess the child as he was paying the 'price' (maintenance). Was it love? Or was it his pound of flesh?

Law[3] requires that the wishes of the child be borne in mind while allowing his/her interim or permanent custody. Children, beyond an age, need to be consulted before any order of their custody is passed. Things cannot be dealt with as per idiosyncrasies of parents who are concerned only about their own emotional needs and feelings of entitlement. Ram Prasad did not understand that simply vilifying Neela and her parents would not get him the custody of the child.

Without realising that his actions were distancing him from his own child, he continued to assert his right to custody, being the biological father. The fact that he needed to build a bond with the child before he could be comfortable in his custody, was beyond Ram Prasad.

3 Sub-section (3) of Section 17, The Guardians and Wards Act, 1890

After this episode, Minku was so traumatised that it would take him ages to get over his fear and anger at being treated in such a manner by his own father.

It is the law of nature that the more you run after something or someone, the more elusive it gets. Ram Prasad's abnormal possessive streak to own his child was driving the child away. The stress to win custody was driving Ram Prasad crazy. On the previous date, I had consciously stopped myself from sizing him up for any signs of schizophrenia. I had told myself not to see him through the glasses of doubt or to start with any such preconception. But he proved that he was insanely obsessive about his own point of view, without caring what the child wanted.

Instances of kidnapping are not unheard of. But this was the first that I encountered. Kidnapping is more common among families settled abroad. Sometimes one parent travels to India with the children on some pretext and does not return; or takes children abroad on the pretext of vacation but does not return. This case was very peculiar.

Parties to the Hague Convention of 25 October 1980 on the Civil Aspects of International Child Abduction (a multilateral treaty developed by the Hague Conference on Private International Law) are under obligation to protect children internationally from the harmful effects of their wrongful removal or retention; and to establish procedures to ensure their prompt return to the State of their habitual residence as well as to secure protection for rights to access. India is neither a signatory to the Convention nor its 1967 Protocol. But, the State Department, USA has accused India of not adhering to the Protocol on International Parental Child Abduction and has claimed that 90 per cent of the requests for the return of abducted children remained unresolved for more than twelve months. The State Department, USA in its latest Annual Report on International Parental Child Abduction (IPCA), described India as a 'non-compliant country', a tag the country carries since 2014 when the first report came out.

In 2017, the State Department, USA reported 104 cases of abduction of children into India. This includes twenty new cases and eighty-four from the previous year. Of course, this data pertains to international abductions. But similar happenings are not uncommon within the country. There are cases aplenty, where children are moved to hostels, residences changed, visitations blocked, and so on, without any intimation to non-custodial parents. Courts are then approached for suitable directions. Even doors of higher courts are knocked for habeas corpus. Such cases are dealt with by the courts considering the peculiarities of facts in each case.

Very recently, the Delhi High Court in a case[4] was compelled to direct issuance of open-ended non-bailable warrants against the father of a minor girl, along with two others, for taking the girl to the UAE (United Arab Emirates) without the court's permission. The mother of the girl had been fighting a custody battle for the minor. As per the plan directed by the court in May 2018, the father was supposed to return the toddler to her mother on 24 August, but he did not do so. Following this, the woman filed a police complaint.

Delhi Police reported that the man fled with the child to

4 Delhi High Court's order dated 1 May 2018 in WP (Crl.) 357/2018 titled Kiran Lohia Vs State & Ors.

West Bengal on 25 August from where he took a taxi to Nepal and that too on a second passport issued by the Commonwealth of Dominica.

The mother, by way of her habeas corpus petition, sought production of her daughter aged about two-and-a-half years.

Keeping in view the contumacious conduct of the child's father, and his scant regard for binding directions, the court besides issuing Non Bailable Warrants (NBWs), also transferred the probe from the Delhi Police to the CBI and directed the agency to probe how they crossed the border despite Look Out Circulars (LOC) being issued against them to ensure they do not travel abroad till they deposit their passports in court.

Ram Prasad had to face the consequences of his act as per criminal law. Such are the desperate actions, distraught parents resort to.

In yet another incident, reported recently in a national daily[5], a man who was appearing in a divorce petition filed by his wife, attacked her outside the courtroom. As soon as he stepped out of the courtroom, he confronted his wife regarding child custody. On her resistance to sharing of custody, an argument ensued and the man pulled out a blade and started attacking his wife on her face and arms. His ten-year-old child was also injured when he tried to intervene. Hearing the wife's calls for help, her lawyer, and a few others rushed out and managed to catch hold of the man and hand him over to the policeman present in the court complex.

---

5 The Times of India, 29 June 2018

Even though the assaulter was caught and was charged under relevant sections of the Indian Penal Code, the child was scarred forever. Besides, the wife had to undergo a minor surgery.

- Narrating details of differences between spouses in a custody petition may not be relevant and may be of no help in securing custody of a child.
- Use of hurtful words for others only brings back hurt to oneself.
- There is nothing wrong in seeking advice from others/family members. But finally, the decision has to be yours because it's your life and you know what is best for you.
- Any act of desperation and any move just to teach your spouse a lesson, is avoidable.
- Any unwarranted and illegal action may not only land you in a soup but also impact the child forever. You may not only lose custody but also have to face criminal proceedings.
- Always remember that any act to hurt and harass the other spouse may only alienate the child further.
- Have faith in the process and the system. In case of any doubt, consult your advocate and well-wishers, who can give a dispassionate opinion.

A Special Child

PARENTS GENERALLY PLAY tug of war for the custody of the child—each pulling the child towards himself/herself with more force than the other—which is quite painful. But I never thought that there could be something more traumatic than that. One foggy January morning, life threw me a curve ball in the guise of Ricky's case. It was an absolutely new life situation for me.

It was heartrending to see that neither of the parents wanted to have the custody of Ricky. It was a chilling day in every sense of the term. The fog outside was dense that winter day but denser was the fog inside. My intellect got clouded, leaving my soul struggling to find a way out. I wished there were a fog light for the soul to find a way out of the quagmire of the life situation, Akash and Suparna had thrown at me.

Ricky's case was a grim reminder that we remain bogged down with our small problems till we meet someone going through a real tough situation.

Akash and Suparna's marriage was over. They had been living separately for more than seven years. Their only child,

Ricky, who was a little different, could have blossomed with the love and acceptance of his own parents.

Ricky, now sixteen, was a special child and was in the custody of Suparna. It was their battle for dissolution of marriage, which had brought them before me. But today, the issue was different. It was about the custody of Ricky.

Both Akash and Suparna blamed each other for Ricky's condition.

'She did not undergo the requisite ultrasound scanning prescribed by the gynaecologist due to her official engagements. It could have saved us from this situation,' Akash said, laying the blame squarely on Suparna.

'It is due to some chromosomal defect, that Ricky is the way he is, and it could not have been detected even through an ultrasound scan,' explained Suparna, while emphasising that Akash would never understand this all his life although this fact had been explained to him by the doctor time and again. 'This was transferred from the 'Y' chromosome,' belaboured Suparna to convince me that Akash was solely responsible for the boy's condition.

'Why would I not have undergone that simple ultrasound...it is me who has been single-handedly bringing up Ricky without much support.'

'From his big shapeless face and peculiar eyes, I knew right from the beginning that he was not a normal child, but Suparna never listened to me. She refused to explore any of the options, which were available at that time. I had even found out from an NGO that there were childless couples abroad who were ready to take the responsibility of a special child but Suparna never agreed. She cannot blame me now. She herself chose to take on the responsibility,' Akash continued with his tirade against Suparna.

I was not surprised at Ricky's condition with so much rejection coming his way since his very birth. What could one expect from the rejected and emotionally deprived child? Such rejection can play havoc even with a normal healthy person. But, a little less than normal Ricky could have blossomed with the love and acceptance of his own parents.

Ricky sat very tense and uptight.

How would one view Ricky if the label of special child was removed for a while and we simply listed a few things he was unable to do?

Neither parent now wanted responsibility for Ricky. My failed efforts at counselling weighed me down. My inability to bring them to any kind of consensus was driving me nuts.

I felt I had been left to handle this life situation on my own (of course, I had the assistance of a counsellor available, if I so needed). It threw at me many questions, which had no straight answers.

What is love? Is it only your physical being that is loved by your dearest ones? If not, why do your own people distance themselves, if your physical being/mind takes a hit? Life is not so simple and linear, I realised. I had tried everything to get the couple to find a solution but failed.

'Should I send Ricky to an orphanage?' was the last arrow I shot at them, hoping to shake Akash and Suparna out of their apathy. I expected a strong reaction from both of them. But nothing of that sort happened. Their silence was more deafening than their words.

'Ma'am, you tell me, how do I handle a teenage boy who is undergoing hormonal changes and needs to be handled by a male?' questioned Suparna with a lump in her throat.

'I can't even accompany him to the toilet...he is a grown up adult now,' she continued. 'When he gets violent, it becomes so difficult to even physically hold him,' she said with tears in her eyes.

'Do you know, he weighs 75 kilograms now! How am I supposed to handle my job and my special child?' asked Suparna, tears rolling down her carefully blushed cheek, leaving a noticeable streak.

'Ma'am if she can't handle him, how am I supposed to handle him with my demanding job,' retorted Akash.

Amidst this fracas, they had lost all sense of decency. Between them they had managed to build so much of rejection for the child.

Our thoughts are a form of energy and reach the person or object, even if they are not put into words. Here both the parents not only created such thoughts but even voiced them vociferously. Ricky was sitting in the last row. Although, this verbal duel may not have been audible to him, I was sure that all the thoughts of 'rejection' were reaching the poor child, who had no control over part of his brain and his motor skills.

Ricky lacked the capacity to articulate his anger at being rejected by his own parents. I could see Ricky fighting tears. He broke down finally. Akash also broke down.

How am I supposed to handle Ricky? You tell me ma'am. I am not used to having a child around. He has been in the exclusive custody of Suparna for more than seven years,' said Akash.

'Did I ever stop you from meeting Ricky and sharing responsibility? Am I responsible for your indifference towards your own child?' questioned Suparna.

'Why should I suffer because you refused to discharge your responsibilities?' asked Suparna, looking straight into Akash's eyes.

Akash was staring at the ground beneath his feet. 'You tell me how he will live with me, when he has never been with me in the last seven years,' asked Akash without raising his eyes.

'I am ready to pay for his caretaker and 50 per cent of the maintenance,' said Akash trying to convince Suparna.

Suparna was not wrong when she said, 'I am now at the verge of collapsing emotionally as well as physically. Ricky has reached puberty. He needs to be told about sexuality and I am at a loss. I don't know how to do that.'

Suparna shared that she felt continually challenged by Ricky's unpredictable behaviour; and that she also felt physically threatened whenever Ricky got out of control.

'Ma'am, I cannot keep a male attendant at home at night, as I live alone. All this stress is affecting not only my health but also my efficiency at work,' said Suparna.

I really did not know what to say!!

I could sense their overwhelming awareness of their limitations in handling not only the complexities of Ricky's affliction, but also of the situation thrown at them.

It is painful to see children deprived of the comfort and security of loving and happy parents. Some children are able to express their suffocation but some are not so expressive. Some turn suicidal, causing further stress to the relational turmoil of parents!

The predicament of Ricky's parents left me with lots of homework to do.

The next date of hearing was more peaceful, but a solution

still eluded us. During chamber counselling both Suparna and Akash though tense were their reformed selves.

'Ma'am, I have found a home run by a reputed NGO which provides day care for such special children,' informed Akash, a little excited.

'What about the night?' was the quick reaction of Suparna.

Suddenly, Akash looked grim. 'Ma'am, you suggest what can be done?' he asked, gazing into my eyes.

What could I suggest, I asked myself. Being parents, they needed to work out a way acceptable to both of them. It was already four o'clock, so the matter was adjourned for the day.

What should they do? The nagging question lingered in my mindscape. Luckily, I was saved from having to make an unpleasant decision. On the next date of counselling, Akash entered my chamber with a spring in his step. He exchanged pleasantries with the court clerk who ushered him in.

Suparna also looked better. They had clearly arrived at a solution, at least for the time being. 'Ma'am, we have decided that Akash will pick up Ricky from my residence every day and drop him at a Home for Special Children. I will pick him up from there in the evening while returning from work,' said Suparna, sounding quite satisfied with this mutually agreed arrangement. She added that Akash had volunteered to pay for Ricky's day-care and for a helping hand at home.

This was a rare instance, when the couple were able to work on the issue and resolve it. Parents at loggerheads simply don't talk to each other; their only communication is in the form of taunts and fault finding. They need to realise that they are not doing any favours to each other; they are doing it only for their child.

It was such a relief for me. It saved me the energy I would have had to invest in finding a solution to their problem—being *parens patriae*, the guardian of the child—had his own parents disowned Ricky.

Such happy endings are rare.

- Life is not simple and linear, but solutions can certainly be found.
- Participation of both the parents in the upbringing of the child means that parents need to contribute as per their capacity—intellectual, emotional, and financial. That is what parents do, when they are together. There cannot be mathematical equal sharing—as the skills and resources of each are different.
- When you dither from taking the responsibility of the child, you are actually creating rejection towards the child—the worst of the emotions.
- Our thoughts are a form of energy and reach the child even if they are not put into words. Beware when you are creating thoughts for the child or the custodial parent.
- Parents are not doing any favours to each other by communicating with each other to find solutions in the best interest of the child.

Obsessed Mother

THAK-THAK. THE loud knock at my chamber door transported me back to the grim reality I was facing. From the intensity of the knock, I gathered that it was not the first knock, and that the person had been knocking for quite some time, while I was lost in reading a file.

'Yesss!' I called out loudly in order to be audible to the person outside. Before I could finish the last syllable, the door was pushed ajar. It seemed that the person was in a great hurry to seek my immediate attention. The next moment, a face peeped inside from the gap, to seek my permission to come in.

It was Aradhna, mother of the child whom I last attended to, earlier in my chamber.

'Ma'am I forgot to draw your attention to a very important fact. My father can come and live with us, if the custody of the child is given to me,' she quickly said, realising that I don't appreciate such interaction once the counselling held in the chamber is over; more particularly, when the other spouse has left.

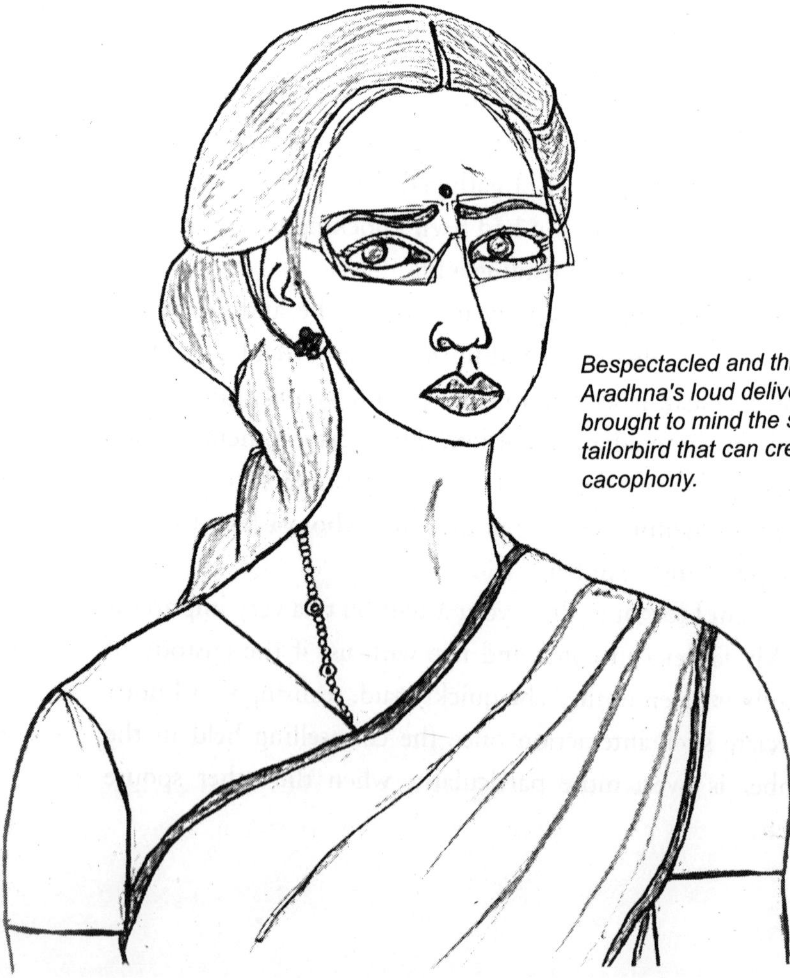

Bespectacled and thin-built Aradhna's loud delivery brought to mind the small tailorbird that can create a cacophony.

'Hmmm!'I just looked at her while nodding my head to assure her that I would keep that fact in mind.

Bespectacled and thin-built, Aradhna was unexpectedly vociferous and her delivery was loud. She reminded me of the small tailorbird that can create a cacophony. The way Aradhna followed up on her petition for her daughter's custody; it seemed to be her full-time job though she was an architect by profession.

Whenever her case was listed for hearing, she would occupy a seat in the last row of chairs in the courtroom at 9:30 am, irrespective of whether her case was to be taken up later in the morning or even past 2 pm. That was not all. After every 10-15 minutes she would walk up to the Reader (Court Clerk) to ask when her case would come up and then go back and sit again. Most of the time, I chose to ignore her presence.

After her hearing, she would continue to sit till I rose for the day, despite being informed that it would take some time to type and sign the order passed in her case. Even thereafter, she would sit in the courtroom or on the bench outside the room. She would not leave the court premises till the last gate was locked. She just wanted to confirm the order passed in her case, though the same was invariably pronounced in the open court and in her presence. This story would repeat on each date of hearing. I found this behaviour very strange. Was she in no hurry to get back to work? I would always wonder.

'What are your office timings?' I asked her once, when I could not suppress my curiosity.

'I am an architect and mostly work from home,' she informed with great pride as if she was assuring me that her presence in court the whole day did not impact her work.

During one of the hearings, Namit, her husband, brought to the court's notice that Aradhna had been removed from service/ asked to resign by three of her previous employers due to her erratic behaviour.

'I had some issues with my employers and resigned. I was not removed,' stated Aradhna dismissively.

Aradhna would not only spend her entire day in court on the date of hearing, but would also be seen in the court for two-three days thereafter. Sometimes she would be there to move miscellaneous applications and on other occasions to collect copies of orders passed on such applications, whether of any significance or not.

Generally, after an order was passed on an application of hers, like for the health report or the school report card of her daughter Anna, she would bring another application to point out that the court had missed some (insignificant) facts or that she wanted to bring another fact on record qua the same prayer.[6]

No amount of explaining that the order on her application had already been passed, and that too in her favour, and therefore a fresh application had no meaning, would work for Aradhna. She would still insist that her application be taken on record.

'You may not issue any notice on this application, as it is only to bring a fact on record,' she would direct the court in a matter-of-fact style. When a notice to the other side, ie. her husband was directed (as is required under law), she would be seen pleading and arguing with the Reader to convince

---

6 prayer: a request contained in a petition to a court for the relief sought by the petitioner.

her that a notice was not required. I would see my Reader's patience giving way. 'You please comply with the court's order and do not bother me,' would be her strict remark to bring the conversation to an end. But, Aradhna would still hang around, totally unaffected by the irritation of the Reader.

Aradhna's life revolved around this litigation and she was literally obsessed with it. Such litigants not only tax themselves but also consume a lot of precious time of the court. To add to that, they are never satisfied with anything.

In stark contrast, Aradhna's husband, most of the time, was represented by an advocate. Namit appeared in court only when his personal presence was required. On such dates also, he would request the hearing be held at 3 pm.

'Ma'am, I am working in a hospital and don't get leave frequently. I can come only after 2 pm,' he would plead.

Anna, their daughter, was in Namit's custody.

Aradhna seemed very technical and arrogant. 'My way' is the only 'right way' seemed to be her philosophy in life. There was no scope for any other viewpoint in her scheme of things. Namit, on the other hand, seemed to have resigned to his fate. He did not respond much to the comments made by Aradhna, unlike other spouses fighting for custody of the child. Generally, spouses pounce upon each other in response to any comment coming their way.

Aradhna's petition for custody contained strange pleadings and stranger accusations unlike the routine wrangling between spouses about the education of the child, lack of time being devoted to the child, etc. Aradhna tried to make out a case for immediate handing over of her daughter's custody to her lest the child's personality be dented for a lifetime, and her education suffer a setback. The documents she annexed with her petition to espouse her cause also made a stark departure from the documents generally filed by spouses.

The first few pages of Aradhna's custody petition were devoted to eulogising her own self and putting down Namit.

When making their case for custody, instead of demonstrating their own worthiness, spouses generally leave no stone unturned to vilify and put the other spouse down.

Aradhna narrated in great detail her upbringing and how she had obliged Namit by marrying him, even ignoring the low financial status of his family. Every aspect of Namit's life was criticised, be it his financial background or his choice of religion, his blind faith in a fitness guru, his peculiar diet fads, his practice of meditation, his dress sense, his sense of hygiene, his leaning towards his parental family, his lack of interest in marital life, etc. It was less about the welfare of the child and more about grabbing an opportunity to show Namit in a poor light.

Anna's skin allergy was attributed to Namit, as was her slow growth and frequent cough and cold, alleging that the same occurred because Namit ignored the child. She alleged that Namit spent all his time in the gym or visiting his dietician, in meditation, or watching television. Aradhna also alleged that Namit lived in his own world, totally oblivious to the needs of Anna.

Aradhna also complained that Anna was forced to meditate; and termed it as a torture of the worst kind. She alleged that such forced meditation was posing a threat to Anna's life and safety. She objected to Namit's 'insensitive and hostile behaviour' towards the child, as she termed it. Aradhna also expressed her apprehension that Namit may pollute the child's mind and turn her hostile towards her.

Other instances of 'cruelty' towards the child inflicted by Namit when they lived together were that Anna was not allowed to have baby food even of a reputed company claiming the same to be synthetic. Aradhna ridiculed Namit for his lack of knowledge. Great emphasis was also laid on the fact that Namit did not allow Anna to be fed milk in a bottle, claiming that it was habit forming; and that Namit did not even permit warming of food in a microwave claiming it to be a health hazard.

Aradhna pointed out that Anna suffered from skin allergy frequently because proper hygiene was not maintained. 'Namit rushes through her bath in the morning; Anna is even made to hurriedly wear the uniform without properly drying her up. She is not given bath on her return from school inspite of her sweating profusely,' went on Aradhna with the long list of reasons behind Anna's skin allergy.

Not providing proper meals to Anna was cited by Aradhna as the main reason of her thin stature. To bring home her point, Aradhna mentioned that at the age of eight, Anna weighed only 20 kilograms.

It was hilarious to look at Aradhna's facial expression when Namit pointed out that Aradhna herself was thin-built and was very skinny when they got married. Involuntarily, I looked at Aradhna and hid a giggle.

To deflect attention, Aradhna started narrating about the care she provided to Anna when she lived with her, like bathing her twice a day after giving her oil massage, cooking a variety of healthy dishes for her, taking her to a nearby park for outings. She boasted that Anna's health showed great improvement and that she had gained weight when she and her father took care of her needs.

Another point Aradhna made was that Anna had to wear braces due to the sheer carelessness of Namit. That was beyond me. How could someone be held responsible for a child's buck teeth and braces. She even attributed Anna's poor eyesight to lack of care on the part of Namit. 'You know Ma'am, Namit is not even aware of the difference between *spherical* and *cylindrical* power. Anna's glasses were in terrible condition when she came to stay with me,' said Aradhna.

Namit's patience gave way at Aradhna's judgmental avalanche, calling him an uncaring, uninformed, and ignorant father. He retorted, 'Ma'am, you can see, she herself is wearing thick glasses. Did her mother also not take care of her? The power of her lenses is more than 5.0 and it is genetic,' he emphasised to point out that Anna's weak eyesight had nothing to do with him.

This time, I could not stop my lips from stretching into a smile, as it was a fact that Aradhna was wearing thick glasses.

Usually each of these cases is replete with eulogising of one's own ways while degrading every bit of the other spouse's handling of the child. This case was a masterpiece, where the wife faulted every aspect of her husband's method of bringing up their daughter and termed his methods as 'orthodox' and 'torturous'. She questioned every belief of his and his way of doing even little things.

This case file had developed some monstrous energy. I came to realise that it caused physical uneasiness within me, the moment I looked at it. Like a sponge, the case file seemed to have absorbed all the negative energy Aradhna and Namit left in the space of the courtroom. The moment their case was called and I opened their file; I could feel turbulent energy, which I am sure also travelled to their own child, whose personality seemed repressed.

'My daughter is being indoctrinated to follow his religious beliefs and to visit his *kuldevta's*[7] temple regularly,' was the rhetoric Aradhna started her submission with, that day. She spewed so much venom and contempt for the priest who headed the temple and Namit's religious beliefs, I am sure, it must have reached Namit though he was not present. Words are after all, nothing but energy, which does travel to the people for whom we create it.

As if what she herself created was not enough, Aradhna would be even seen consulting, outside the courtroom, another very vociferous and aggressive mother, who apprehended that her husband was about to remove their child out of the jurisdiction of the court to a new life and culture in USA. These two cases were different from other custody cases, which involved routine wrangles of parents over interim custody, residence of children during vacation, their schooling, etc.

Seeing Aradhna and other such parents, whose cases become their life mission, I also realised how smartly these parents even acquired legal vocabulary and learnt the procedures of law to combat each other.

Interestingly, Aradhna had gathered a large number of documents about Namit's Kuldevta's temple and its head priest, thanks to the Internet. She had even made a collage of newspaper clippings about that temple, its head priest, and its

7 clan deity; an ancestral tutelary deity in Hinduism, who is the object of one's devotion in order to have the god watch over one's family and children from probable misfortune.

goings on, critical review et al. So much for gaining custody of the child! But not a word about her own suitability, except her educational qualifications and self-praise that she was a caring and devoted mother.

Aradhna had also mentioned in her petition that when she got Anna's braces checked by her doctor, she was told that they were doing more harm to her teeth than correcting the defect. There was no stopping Aradhna after she read out the relevant paragraph of the doctor's report. She alleged that Namit had not bothered to get the braces changed. She claimed that Anna's personal hygiene was also not taken care of. Her undergarments were filthy when she visited her the last time. She also mentioned that Namit made Anna use the same set of undergarments for a year irrespective of their condition.

'Namit hasn't inculcated in Anna the habit of brushing her teeth in a proper manner because of which Anna has developed caries and cavities,' was yet another complaint.

'Even the hair brush Anna uses is meant for elders and not for an eight-year-old girl,' went on Aradhna.

What was amusing was that in support Aradhna had filed photographs of Anna posing with her undergarments to show their condition and also holding her socks up in the air, in the next picture. Aradhna even filed, with her petition, photographs of Anna's hair brush and spectacles. It not only seemed insanely funny but also revealed the dark side of her personality that Aradhna herself was not aware of. She was well intentioned but did not know the damage she was doing to herself and to the child by using the child for displaying the evidence. I was saddened as well as amused at the amount of energy and effort she put into collecting those pieces of 'evidence'.

I suddenly developed goose bumps. A little introspection revealed the reason. I found myself trying to recollect when I had last checked my son's nails, undergarments, and spectacles, and whether he was actually brushing his teeth properly every morning. A wave of fright swept through me at the thought of being deprived of the custody of my son on these grounds. I was relieved the next moment, when I realised that he was already eighteen years old and could choose to be with me if he so desired.

In the evening, when I reached home, my son caught me looking at his hands. 'Why are you staring at me?' he asked. I was actually looking at his nails, and was shocked to see dirt under his long nails.

'Am I not a good mother?' I questioned myself.

'Now, do not start with your lecture please,' he reacted. 'Don't disturb me. I am in the middle of Star Wars,' he pleaded.

I left his room, as I did not want to disturb him while he was busy with a favourite video game. I knew he would not pay any attention at that time. While leaving his room, his shoes and socks strewn near his bed caught my attention. 'Mom, now don't start with shoes please...I will put them in the shoe rack,' he begged.

'How would Anna have felt while posing to show her nails, while holding her socks in the air to demonstrate their filth,' I wondered. What impact such behaviour of a parent has on the child's impressionable mind, calls for a serious study. To me it felt like an accused holding his nameplate giving details of the crime he allegedly committed.

To demonstrate that she loved her husband Namit and brought him gifts, Aradhna had filed photographs of cuff links, neck ties, blazers, flip flops, and other toiletries that she brought him from her trips abroad. She also filed a photograph of a digital notepad, which she had gifted to Namit. She even filed pictures of the books she had gifted him while they lived together. All this made me wonder whether Aradhna was taking photographs and preserving them to produce as evidence at the right time.

What I found very disturbing was an audio CD filed by Aradhna, which contained a conversation between herself and Anna, in support of her plea that Anna was being ill-treated by her father and his family members. The said conversation was in question-answer form. Aradhna put a question to Anna to which she responded. Aradhna claimed that Anna had categorically stated in this conversation that she loved her and wanted to stay with her; and that she was beaten up by Namit.

Close scrutiny of the transcript revealed that Aradhna had put very suggestive and leading questions to the poor child, Anna, and she had no other way but to respond in a manner favouring Aradhna. Here is a glimpse of the said conversation:

Aradhna: Do you miss mummy?

Anna: Yes

Aradhna: Who else do you miss?

Anna: Silence.

Aradhna: Do papa, bua (paternal aunt), or dada (paternal grandfather) beat you?

Anna: Silence.

Aradhna: Do they get angry when you talk to me?

Anna: No.

Aradhna: Does bua threaten you?

Anna: Sometimes.

Aradhna: You don't worry. I will get your custody; then no one can scold you. You will not be threatened here if you come and stay with me.

Anna: Hmmm.

Aradhna: Would you like to stay with me? Say yes or no.

Anna: Okay.

Aradhna: Why don't you say yes or no?

Anna: Silence.

Aradhna: Did papa slap you for talking to me?

Anna: No.

Aradhna: Do you cry when you are slapped?

Anna: Yes, once I cried.

Aradhna: Who slapped—papa, bua, or dada?

Anna: No one.

Aradhna: Just now you told that you were slapped?

Anna: Silence.

Aradhna: Didn't papa say anything to dada?

Anna: No

Aradhna: Didn't papa stop you from crying?

Anna: No

Aradhna: Did papa also beat you?

Anna: I don't remember.

Aradhna: Why?

Anna: Silence.

Aradhna: Why did you not phone me, when he hit you?

Anna: I don't remember.

Aradhna: You don't remember anything. Are you not taking almonds?

Anna: They are finished.

Aradhna: Does bua also beat you?

Anna: No. She only scolds me.

Aradhna: Were you beaten or scolded?

Anna: I don't remember.

Aradhna: When I call you on the phone, does your papa tell you to tell me that you are in a hurry or you have to go to play with friends?

Anna: Hmmm. I don't know.

Aradhna: Is anyone standing near you?

Anna: What?

Aradhna: Does he ask you to tell a lie?

Anna: Don't know.

Aradhna: You are lying to me?

Anna: I am not lying.

Aradhna: You are not answering properly?

Anna: I've got to play now.

Aradhna: Are you asked to meditate?

Anna: Yes.

Aradhna: How many times in a day?

Anna: Don't remember.

Aradhna: Are you made to sit for mediation in the morning and evening?

Anna: Only in the evening.

Aradhna: Everyday?

Anna: No

Aradhna: Not daily?

Anna: No.

Aradhna: Do you meditate on school days also?

Anna: No. Only on holidays.

Aradhna: All holidays?

Anna: Don't remember.

Aradhna: What do you take for lunch?
Anna: Burger.
Aradhna: Everyday?
Anna: No.
Aradhna: What do you take in your tiffin on other days?
Anna: I don't remember.
Aradhna: Do you eat vegetables?
Anna: No. Sometimes.
Aradhna: Dry fruit must be there at home?
Anna: They are finished.
Aradhna: Finished?
Anna: When I ask papa, he does not bring.
Aradhna: You do not get dry fruit? And do you eat fruits?
Anna: No.
Aradhna: Papa does not ask you to eat fruit everyday?
Anna: Sometimes I eat.
Aradhna: Why?
Anna: Acha. Bye.
Aradhna: Does papa see what are you taking in your tiffin?
Anna: Sometimes. Ok bye.
Aradhna: What happened? Is anyone standing near you?
Anna: Bye
Aradhna: Don't be scared. Tell me.
Anna: Bye.
Aradhna: Okay. We will talk tomorrow.
Anna: Ok. May I go now?
Aradhna: We will talk tomorrow.
Anna: Okay

I found it horrifying. This kind of conversation would have

put even an adult under stress. Aradhna had tried to extract information from Anna by trapping her. In my opinion, it was plain and simple torture inflicted upon the child by an adult. Aradhna does not fit the image of a tormentor one usually has in mind. In her own perspective, Aradhna was deeply concerned about Anna's well-being. She did not realise how she was impacting the child's personality forever. I passed directions to both the parents to refrain from putting such queries to Anna and recording any conversation with her.

As if the trauma of constant conflict between the parents was not enough, Aradhna unknowingly inflicted further wounds on the psyche of the poor child.

Such childhood wounds, traumas, and feelings remain trapped unless consciously addressed and released. Traumas block the free flow of energy and the wounds direct their lives and relationships. Children carry toxicity, shame, and guilt, which do not actually belong to them. They develop unhealthy behavioural patterns if such old traumas, anger, pain, and other similar feelings are not released.

Anna, I felt, was tied up in a bind due to her parents' beliefs.

It is quite a task to heal the inner wounded child, when we grow up.

The peculiar characters of this case travelled home with me. My efforts to deconstruct the whole gamut of facts and the personalities really weighed me down sometimes, as if I bore the cross of their emotional entanglement around my neck.

'Was I getting too much into their emotional hotchpotch and karma?' I questioned myself. I consciously stepped back and reminded myself to simply be a witness to the dramas, which unfolded in the court.

Aradhna made every effort to demonstrate that Anna suffered in academics due to lack of proper supervision and support by Namit. Being an architect, she was better equipped to help Anna in academics. I got tired of listening to her discourses on the significance of scientific temper in one's life; and how important it was to have a strong foundation in education.

With excruciating frankness and even at the risk of being misunderstood (in Family Court you always run that risk, as both the sides feel that they are not being understood), I had to tell Aradhna that she was harming Anna by talking negatively about her and her environment all the time.

I thought Anna's personal and social adjustment was more important at this juncture than the display of her ability to perform in academics and other extracurricular activities. What would be the purpose of high intellectual performance if the child were not stable emotionally? I think bringing up a child to be a balanced person is more important than creating an emotionally volatile person with academic excellence.

The real issues between Aradhna and Namit, as I could sense over a period of time, were the differences in their opinions about most aspects of life. Aradhna did not share Namit's views and opinions about food, clothes, manner of bringing up a child etc. She was absolutely intolerant of Namit's religious beliefs and everything connected with it. She was totally against his fitness guru and complained about the time Namit spent in meditation.

Aradhna seemed unaware that research after research has proved that meditation helps a person to connect with himself and to attain focus in life. Could this be justified as a ground for snatching the custody of the child from Namit? I asked myself.

Recently, I came across a novel method evolved by a school to deal with truant children. Instead of handing out a punishment of detention or suspension from class, to an unruly child, the Robert W Coleman Elementary School in USA has been doing something different when students act out. They offer meditation to such children. Instead of punishing disruptive kids or sending them to the principal's office, the Baltimore school has something called the 'Mindful Moment Room' instead. The room looks nothing like the standard windowless detention room. Instead, it is filled with lamps, decorations, and plush purple pillows. Misbehaving kids are encouraged to sit in the room and go through practices like breathing or meditation, helping them calm down and re-centre. They are also asked to talk through what happened. Meditation and mindfulness have been found to be more effective scientifically.

Interestingly, recently at the Centre for Healthy Minds at the University of Wisconsin – Madison, USA, researchers have found that meditative practice may be associated with slowed biological aging. They studied the brains of about 105 adults from Madison, Wisconsin, who became the control group.

A Buddhist monk, Yongey Mingyur Rinpoche (YMR), a renowned meditation practitioner and teacher, who began meditating at the age of nine also underwent BrainAGE analysis. In the study, researchers used structural MRI to scan the brain of YMR four times over the course of fourteen years, starting from when he was twenty-seven years old.

The analysis showed that YMRs brain had delayed aging in comparison with the control group, who fell onto the 'typical aging band'. The analysis also showed that YMR's forty-one-year-old brain actually resembled that of a thirty-three-year-old.

Research has proved that meditation helps a person to connect with himself and to attain focus in life.

Richard J Davidson, the Founder & Director of the Center for Healthy Minds noted that the brain of the Tibetan Monk, who spent more than 60,000 hours of his life in formal meditation, aged more slowly than the brains of those in the control group.

Although, no firm conclusion has been drawn, there is growing evidence that meditative practice may slowdown biological aging.

Interestingly the impact of meditation has also been studied amongst prisoners. The documentary film *The Dhamma Brothers* chronicles the spiritual evolution of a group of convicts who participated in a Vipassana meditation. Stunning transformation was noticed in these hardened offenders over time as shared in Alan Cohen's book, *A Course In Miracles Made Easy* scribed by Helen Schucman.

The book also shares that on a broader scale, studies indicate that when one per cent of people in a city meditate regularly, the violent crime rate in that city drops. In 1993, a large group of meditators went to Washington, DC (known as the murder capital of the United States), to establish greater peace in that city. Soon thereafter the murder rate declined. More than 200 similar experiments have been conducted in schools and prisons around the world, with astounding results. The book further shares that when meditation was introduced into prison programs in Senegal two penitentiaries were ultimately closed.[8]

Regarding different religious practices adopted by spouses, recently, I came across an interview of accomplished artist and leading Bollywood actor, Naseeruddin Shah. Shah, a Muslim,

8 Brief overview can be seen on YouTube 'The Square Root of One Per Cent'.

is married to Ratna Pathak, a Hindu. When the interviewer asked him what religion his children followed, Shah gave a very profound reply. He shared that when he was asked by the school authorities why he had left blank the column meant for 'religion' in their school admission forms, he told them that he wanted his children to choose their religion. He did not want to choose Islam or Hinduism for them; he did not want to impose his choice on them.

Does a spouse lose his/her right to practice any religious belief after marriage, I asked myself.

It was strange to see that differences in religious and other beliefs of spouses could be made a ground for depriving a parent of the custody of the child. Both Aradhna and Namit perhaps needed to see not only a counsellor but also a doctor or a person of scientific temperament, who could explain to them the facts as they were, whether it was processed child food or the effect of warming food in the microwave, or whether bottle-feeding is habit forming.

'Anna is being forced to sit for mediation and chant mantras. Such forced thoughts are dangerous for young Anna,' complained Aradhna, looking extremely worried.

'He inflicts atrocities on the child to make her toe the line,' went on Aradhna.

I counted my blessings to have (almost) never been questioned about my beliefs and opinions about food, way of bathing, bringing up my children, the kind of medical treatment—allopathy or homeopathy—I chose for my children and myself.

Until I was confronted with this litigation, I had not known what I was blessed with. Since then I have made it a ritual to count my blessings.

This case was also an important encounter with certain realities of life. Otherwise, I could not have imagined the propensity of the impact such aspects of life, can have on one's family life. Of course, I had heard about minor conflicts in families regarding religious beliefs; and had also heard about a particular approach to bringing up of the child, being commented upon, but no farther.

Strangely, Aradhna blamed Namit even for Anna's bad handwriting. No doubt, a parent needs to help the child improve his/her handwriting, but does the lack of it make a person a bad parent? I know many people who have an awful handwriting, but are beautiful human beings.

Bill Gates, Beethoven, Abraham Lincoln, and even the Father of our Nation did not have a great handwriting.

Aradhna's case was an eye-opener for me making me realise how normal and loving human beings can turn not only cold and hurtful to others, but also, become narcissistic, if the other does not conform to their way of leading life. They can go to any extent, even at the cost of their own peace and in total disregard of the child's well-being, to simply deprive the other spouse of custody.

Anna's stunted growth was a grim reminder of how the overhang of parental authority can stifle the natural blooming of a child. Parents' race to create perfect children is what hurts them the most.

Words have immense power to inspire you or destroy you. For a small child, the parents' words are gospel truth. Therefore words deriding the child can damage the child for a lifetime. Aradhna mindlessly commented on Anna's traits not realising the impact her words/comments had on her.

While deciding custody matters, the court has to primarily consider the welfare of the child and give due weightage to all the circumstances such as the child's ordinary comfort and contentment, her intellectual, moral, and physical development, her health, education, general maintenance, etc. Apart from that, the court has also to give due weightage to emotional considerations.

The Hon'ble Supreme Court in a number of cases has observed that the role of the mother has greater importance than that of the father during the formative years of a child. It is considered that the mother can take better care of the physical, biological, and psychological growth of a young child unless the mother suffers from any disqualification.

In this case, the mother herself needed counselling and the child had been in the father's custody. But, Anna seemingly had been alienated from the father by Aradhna's constant feeding of negativity.

Aradhna succeeded in obtaining the custody of Anna by the order of the higher court. As Anna in her interaction with the court expressed a desire to live with her mother, the custody was shifted to Aradhna. This whole process of brain washing, programming, and alienating a child from the other parent, is termed as 'Parent Alienation Syndrome', a term coined in 1980 by a popular American child psychiatrist, Dr Richard A Gardner.

The term 'parental alienation' refers to attempts by one parent to alienate the children from the other parent, using psychological pressure of several kinds. It may be used during a marriage or resorted to after separation when fighting over custody.

Jennifer Harman, a Colorado State University social psychologist, who studies parental alienation and its consequences, noted that it can be caused both directly and indirectly. She and her co-authors have published new research showing that mothers and fathers use slightly different tactics when engaging in these destructive behaviours. Her latest analysis, published in the *Journal of Family Violence* examines gender differences in many types of alienating behaviours. The study includes the work of her co-authors Demosthenes Lorandos, a Michigan-based legal scholar, Zeynip Biringen, a professor in the CSU Department of Human Development and Family Studies, and Caitlyn Grubb, a psychology graduate student.

Harman distinguishes between direct and indirect aggression. She says direct aggressions can include instances when the alienating parent hits the targeted parent at child exchange time. The alienating parent may also block parenting time with the child; send hostile emails and texts to the targeted parent; block or change phone numbers so that the targeted parent cannot reach the child; and make unilateral decisions about the child, in violation of court orders.

In contrast, indirect aggression can include instances when the alienating parent badmouths the targeted parent to the child or turns friends and family against the targeted parent. The alienating parent usually tells the children false stories from the past about the targeted parent and often yells at the targeted parent in front of the children.

Such behaviour many a times succeeds in damaging the child's relationship with the targeted parent. It can create what social psychologists call an 'enmeshed identity' with the alienator, resulting in the child essentially acting as a proxy for the perpetrator.

Alienated children's acting out on behalf of the perpetrator is another form of direct aggression against the targeted parent. According to Harman, 'Indirect behaviours are more circuitous.'

'Alienators lie to manipulate, spread rumours, and make false claims. Such claims might be grounded in truth, but details are twisted or exaggerated and can be challenging for a custody evaluator to unravel,' says Harman.[9]

- Experience tells that custody petitions are more about showing the other down.
- Instead of counting negatives of the child and the spouse in whose custody the child is, focus more on what you can provide.
- By pointing out the negatives of the child in order to secure custody, a parent may despite good intentions cause damage to the child's health—mental/psychological/physical. The parents' words, for a small child, are gospel truth and form the child's image of herself.
- Such childhood wounds, traumas, and feelings remain trapped in their being unless consciously addressed and released. Children carry for a lifetime such toxicity, shame, and guilt which do not actually belong to them.
- Children develop unhealthy behavioural patterns if such old traumas, anger, pain, and other similar feelings are not released.
- Such wounds may even direct their lives and relationships.

9 Delhi Times, ANI, The Times of India, 23 November 2019

- There is hardly any point in achieving a high intellectual performance if the child is not stable emotionally.
- Focus on your own issues rather than consulting everyone visiting the court. Such consultations may add to your confusion, instead of showing you the way.
- Making litigation your life purpose is surely avoidable.

Tug of War

I COULD NOT recognise him at first glance. He had put on a lot of weight. Surprisingly, his weight was spread evenly all over. His cheeks were as bloated as his tummy. Aarav also seemed a little stressed.

'Do you want to share something with me?' I asked. 'No,' he replied in a monosyllable.

'You wanted to see me, I was told,' he said after a short pause.

I simply said yes and did not add anything further.

At the previous court hearing when Aashima, Aarav's mother, had insisted on a meeting with Aarav, his father's advocate had insisted that I interact with Aarav before I permit any such meeting. He claimed that Aarav did not wish to see his mother anymore.

Though Aashima and Aniket had been living separately for the past two-three years, they had not filed for divorce. There was no litigation pending between the two of them, except

Aniket's petition for custody/guardianship of Aarav. Aarav was in Aashima's custody when they separated. Later, during the pendency of the custody case, at Aarav's insistence, Aashima allowed him to live with his father for some time. But he continued to stay with his father.

Aarav had the company of his cousins and grandparents at his dad's place. It seemed as if he was pampered by his grandparents.

Aashima had not seen Aarav for the past three months and wanted to meet him. She had broken down when the advocate said Aarav did not want to see her. Aashima begged that she be allowed to meet Aarav at least for an hour, to see how he was doing.

Aarav perhaps did not know that it was his father's desire that I meet him before deciding on his mom's request for regular visitation.

Warring parents often play tug of war with their children not seeing the intense damage they are causing.

'Have you met your Mom?' I asked Aarav.

'Yes,' was his irritated reply.

'But why have you called me to meet her?' he questioned me.

'Do you not want to meet her?' I asked him.

'No,' was his emphatic reply.

I was taken aback by his reaction.

I started asking Aarav about his cousins just to break the tension, which had built during the first few minutes of this conversation.

When Aarav lived with his mother, he used to resist visiting his father. Now, when he was with his father, he was not interested in meeting his mother. I was still trying to figure out why he did not want to meet his mom now.

'Ma'am it becomes very hectic for me,' he said, before I could ask him more.

'*Kabhi papa ko sambhalo!! Kabhi mummy ko sambhalo!!* (Take care of papa, take care of mummy) I cannot take it anymore. I get very tired,' he said.

'I just want to stay with papa now and don't want to meet my mom,' he announced with finality. Aarav's distraught face conveyed his misery. It was a signal to leave the issue for a while. I asked him about his school activities and interests trying to calm him down.

'Haven't you gained weight Aarav?' I asked.

'No,' he said. Aarav was just thirteen years but looked like he weighed 100 kilograms

'Ma'am I am just as I was when I went to stay with papa,' he tried to convince me. It had been ten months since he went to his father's house.

'Don't you think you need to address it?' I asked with concern.

'I am trying to work on it,' Aarav assured me.

'You know, I lost my mother about three months ago and I miss her very much,' I shared this fact with Aarav, to strike a personal chord with him.

'Oh! I am so sorry Ma'am,' Aarav's demeanour changed completely.

'What happened,' he asked with great concern, very unlike a child of his age.

His simple concern touched a raw nerve inside me.

I was transported to my own world and remembered how we took our mother for granted. We fought with her, argued with her, got irritated with her habit of constantly pestering us to eat something or the other when we visited her for a short duration. But she hardly paid any heed to our entreaties. That was her way of expressing her love, I now realise. I was also reminded how she would call up and enquire about some small little ailment or pain we might have mentioned to her. That ailment may have left us and we may have completely forgotten about it but she never forgot to enquire about it.

'How could this child feel so burdened about keeping in touch with his mother,' I tried to fathom.

Aarav's response to my query on why he did not feel like meeting his mother was a great lesson, if warring parents could hear.

'Ma'am she will start asking a thousand questions, the moment she meets me,' was his haggard reply.

'I know she will start with her *rona dhona* (emotional drama), the moment we meet...Oh I miss you and all that...! I can't take it anymore. I want to stay with papa and don't want to meet mom.'

'When I was with mom, I did not want to talk to papa

The real cause of Aarav's obesity was the emotional upheaval he was undergoing in his life.

or visit him, you remember Ma'am?' He looked askance and paused to check if I remembered.

'It becomes very difficult for me to stay with one and to interact with the other,' he said with melancholy in his voice.

Recently, a national daily[10] reported that a fifteen-year-old boy, in a letter to the President, sought 'permission' to end his life due to the strained relations between his parents. His father was a government official. His mother worked at a bank. In his letter, forwarded to the Prime Minister's Office, the boy is said to have expressed his exasperation over the nasty quarrels between his parents and claimed that it was having an adverse effect on his studies. He had also alleged that his father, who was suffering from cancer, was being 'threatened by anti-social elements' at the behest of his mother. Disgusted with the situation, the boy wanted to end his life, officials claimed.

This is the magnitude of trauma which some warring parents heap on the child.

Parents, who become an emotional burden for a child, should sit up and introspect. But warring spouses are hardly able to look at the child's perspective. They are wallowing and drowning in their own emotional pain. Their interaction with the child is coloured with their own hurt and emotional trauma for which they blame the other spouse.

I think Aarav had evolved his own way of protecting himself and his personal space. His aggression seemed to be his way of saying 'you cannot burden me with your emotional load, while I am trying to manage my own self between the two of you'.

---

10 Times Nation, The Times of India dated 18 July 2019

Aarav's story played in my sub-conscious for a long time. I tried to mentally deconstruct the complexities a single child goes through while being a part of the triangle.

During further conversations while trying to find some way to persuade Aarav to see his mother for a while, from his body language, I realised that I was suspect of veering him towards some alternate arrangement. I had no option but to change the course of my conversation.

'How did you come to live with papa?' I asked Aarav.

'Mom used to keep threatening me that if I did not listen to her she would call mama/nana (maternal uncle/grandfather). Whether I played video games, or listened to music for long, or watched a movie, everything irritated her,' he said.

'Ma'am I am improving in my studies now. I need to improve my grades in science and math and I am taking tuitions. I do not want to be disturbed,' he announced in no uncertain terms.

'Please don't ask me to meet her again,' pleaded Aarav, before I could say something. 'Who are mama and nana to scold me? They are not my parents!!' said Aarav.

'Did you make efforts for a patch-up between your parents?' I asked.

'Ma'am I did try initially. But could not help,' he shared.

'They cannot stay together, I know,' he made it clear that he understood.

I was not sure if Aashima would ever understand why Aarav did not want to see her. She would not be able to handle the feeling of rejection and the consequent pain, I was sure. It is very difficult to explain to parents that such a reaction of the child has nothing to do with them. It simply reflects the child's inability to handle the situation they are put in.

Aarav was no stranger to the aftermath of such a situation. Previously, when he lived with his mother and visited his father occasionally, he was made to see a psychologist/counsellor, a number of times, as his conduct was termed as a *behavioural problem* by his school teacher.

Aarav had shared with me that he was branded a 'thief' by his paternal aunt, when he took away an X-box from his father's house while visiting him. While living with his mother, by court's order, Aarav used to visit his father on Sundays every fortnight. His father lived in a joint family consisting of Aarav's paternal aunt and uncle, their children, and his grandparents.

The joint family home had an exclusive room for children with all electronic devices like home theatre, video games, X-box, etc.

The joint family home had an exclusive room for children with all electronic devices like home theatre, video games, X-box, etc. Aarav really looked forward to playing these games and watching movies on the home theatre with his cousins. On one such visit, while returning to his mother's place, Aarav took away the X-box without informing Aniket. Aniket alleged that he had stolen it because of Aashima's bad influence. Aashima had told Aarav that his father had called him a thief. This hurt Aarav deeply and he stopped visiting his father.

It was not surprising to hear that Aashima even started receiving complaints from Aarav's school about his erratic behaviour. Both the parents were called by the school principal and Aarav was recommended for counselling by a child psychologist.

'I never liked that pug-faced counsellor. She only passed time by asking me funny questions and making me tell stories,' shared Aarav with contempt.

'How could I explain something I had never done,' asked Aarav.

'When I never stole anything and never misbehaved with anyone, where was the occasion for me to correct myself, you only tell me aunty,' asked Aarav.

I was acutely aware of his gaze. I had no ready answer to satisfy him.

Aarav had earlier been taken to doctors for his unmanageable weight. I feel doctors only talk about the food and chemicals (medicines) that lead to obesity. I doubt whether any of them addressed the real issue of the emotional upheaval that Aarav was going through. Even his own parents did not realise that the fault lay with them and not with the child.

Deeper conversations with Aarav revealed the load of his

unmet/unattended emotions and fears, which no one could understand. He had his own private world to which no one had access. He had many fears and expectations that may seem unreal to us but were the real emotions of an insecure, growing teenager.

I cautioned myself against getting too entangled in his emotional mishmash lest I lose the objectivity required to deal with his life situation. Showing excessive sympathy could be counterproductive, as Aarav had to go back to his own home and live with the same people and deal with the same relationships.

Virginia M Axline, in her book *Dibs In Search Of Self*, has shared the tale of the emergence of a strong, healthy personality in a previously deeply disturbed child. *Dibs In Search Of Self* is the story of a child in search of self, revealed through the process of psychotherapy. Virginia writes:

> 'The value of any successful therapeutic experience, in my opinion, depends upon the balance that is maintained between what the individual brings into the sessions and what he takes out. If the therapy becomes the predominant and controlling influence in the individual's daily life, then I would have serious doubts as to its effectiveness. I wanted Dibs to feel that he had the responsibility to take away with him his increasing ability to assume responsibility for himself and thus gain his psychological independence.'

Though the role of a Family Court Judge is quite distinct from that of a psychotherapist, Virginia's wisdom certainly comes as a great guidance.

Aashima and Aniket were not able to figure out why Aarav's

grades were slipping. Their search for the reasons outside was meaningless. They needed to look within. They could hardly sense Aarav's mental condition. The fears and loneliness, which he felt in both homes, reverberated throughout the counselling sessions. I had no doubt in my mind that it was the parents who needed counselling. They needed to understand his condition and open a channel of communication between them and their child. They needed to sincerely discuss Aarav's concerns and the issues he faced, instead of voicing their respective conflicts and blaming each other for the situation they were in.

Aarav's case, as usual, was the case of the child caught in the war between the parents. Neither of the parents had shown the maturity to keep the child out of their mutual differences. They failed in their duty to ensure that the child was the least impacted.

- Do not interrogate the child on his return after meeting the non-custodial parent.
- Do not burden the child with your own emotional download; it may impact the child's emotional health forever.
- Do not take a child's refusal to meet you as your rejection. It may simply reflect his/her own inability to handle the situation she is put in, ie. to choose between either of the parents. The child may simply be dealing with her own hurt and emotional turmoil and protecting her space.

- Many a times, it is the parents, who need counselling.
- Parents need to sincerely address the child's concerns and issues instead of voicing their respective conflicts and blaming each other for the situation. They should make an effort to view issues from the child's perspective.

A WAY OUT

'Now don't cry like a girl! Be a man!'
His father told him the truth of the land.
The thirteen-years-old's heart was engraved.
He knew at that moment that boys are brave.
Only when he turned twenty-nine,
He could tell that it was all a lie.
It was the first time he heard his daughter cry.
His little girl's the strongest, told his eyes.
Things started to go out of shape.
Guess life doesn't always go a man's way.
The baggage he got from his father years ago,
Was now too heavy for him to hold,
Sinking deeper with the broken ties,
Depression got the better of his life.
Now when his daughter was five,
Just to see her face would take him a lifetime.
Guess it's not always a woman who suffers.
Fathers too have the heart of a mother.
Inside he cries when hurt,
Because the 'man' too was a 'child' once.

—Ishita Pandey

VAIBHAV'S SOFT FEATURES and charming eyes would have turned even a stone-hearted person into a marshmallow. His brown pants impeccably matched the pink full-sleeved shirt he wore. The brown and pink silver cuff links, which held the two sides of his sleeves together, could hardly be missed.

Vaibhav went into depression after he lost the custody battle for his daughter Sanya. But he was fortunate to have the love and support of his family and friends. Though Vaibhav and Gayatri were still contesting a divorce petition, Vaibhav, to fill up the void and fulfil his desire to bring up and nurture a child, went in for surrogacy. He was blessed with a daughter. He gave his daughter, a similar sounding name—Sanora. Deep satisfaction was plainly evident from the big smile he flashed when I met him last.

'I got a second chance to be a dad,' he announced with pride.

She cannot succeed in driving me mad,' he said with élan.

I was happy for him. Because, it is painful to see a life sink into the pit of depression.

'But I still miss Sanya very much,' he shared.

'I am looking forward to introducing Sanora to Sanya. I am sure she will be very excited to meet her,' said Vaibhav, a childlike brilliance illuminating his face.

Vaibhav's revelation of being blessed with a daughter through surrogacy wreaked havoc in court. Gayatri turned more vitriolic the moment she came to know about the child. The fact that the child's name was similar to Sanya's, added fuel to the fire. Her entire being shook with anger and she became incoherent. She threatened Vaibhav in open court that she would not let him live in peace and would take legal recourse against his resorting to surrogacy without her consent, while their marriage was yet to be dissolved.

'How could you do it without my consent?' screamed Gayatri at the top of her voice.

'I did not need your permission,' pat came the reply from Vaibhav, who till then was maintaining a peaceful exterior.

'You cannot on the one hand disallow me to meet our daughter and at the same time object to my having a surrogate child to fulfil my nurturing needs,' went on Vaibhav without losing his cool.

This case brought home to me, how strong the urge to have one's own child and satisfy one's parental instinct could be.

'How could you…? What do you think of yourself…? You cannot take law into your own hands. I will not leave you till the end. I will ensure that you are punished for this lowly act of yours,' threatened Gayatri.

I let her vent her strong emotions, lest she suffer in any other manner. From the verbal assault let loose by Gayatri on Vaibhav and her demeanour, it was obvious that she felt belittled as if her existence did not matter to Vaibhav. Her rhetoric of Vaibhav cheating on her, indulging in uncivilised behaviour, etc. was nothing but the outburst of a wounded ego. She was shaken out of the belief that she could torture Vaibhav by depriving him of Sanya's custody and making him beg for even short meetings with his daughter. She felt empowered by the child by her side. She could take revenge for her perceived ill treatment at the hands of Vaibhav and his family members. Now, she stood deprived of *the tool* she had been using to inflict torture on Vaibhav. The entire world she had created around their only child Sanya had fallen apart.

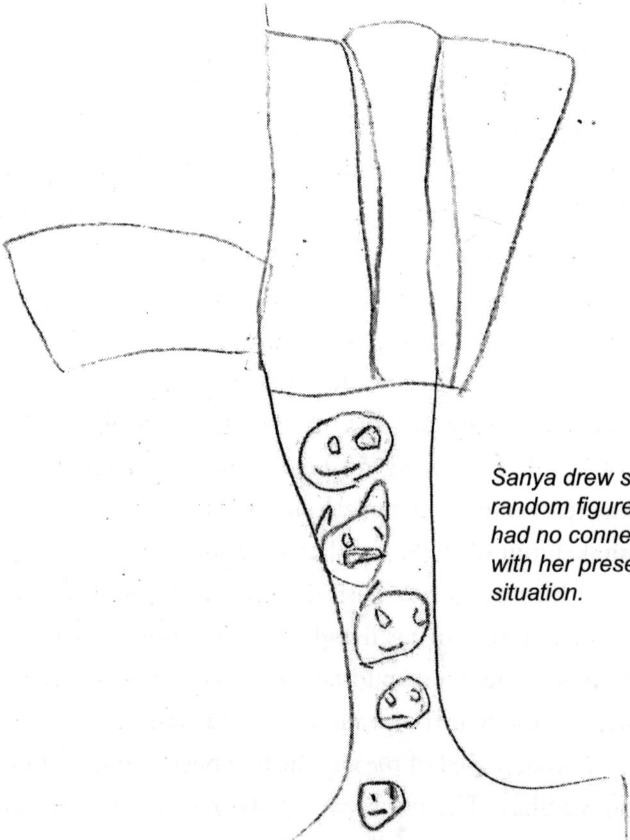

Sanya drew some random figures, which had no connection with her present situation.

Both, Gayatri and Vaibhav, were well educated, employed, and had the means to look after Sanya. Sanya was about five years old and had expressed a desire to be with Gayatri and her family including cousins, so the court had given her custody to Gayatri. Vaibhav was initially allowed to meet Sanya every Sunday for about three hours. Gayatri tried to scuttle these meetings, sometimes taking the child out of Delhi on the pretext of an excursion, sometimes on account of illness, sometimes due to some family function and so on. After every such stalled meeting, Vaibhav would file a contempt petition. Gayatri would invariably plead the genuineness of the grounds on which the child could not meet Vaibhav. Such petitions would be disposed of by consensus, with Gayatri giving an undertaking not to take the child out on Sundays or to intimate Vaibhav in advance about any illness, so that he could visit the ailing child.

Despite the court's regular intervention, Vaibhav's common refrain was that Gayatri made every meeting with Sanya unpleasant. She would find different ways to ruin the meetings, finding fault with everything whether it was the duration of the meeting, the pick-up and drop-off of the child, the place of meeting, etc. Finally, Vaibhav gave up, as he did not want Sanya to suffer anxiety every time they met.

Vaibhav was now very happy. Even Sanya, during a chamber meeting, seemed excited to meet her sibling. She couldn't care less about what her mother thought of the whole affair.

During an interaction in the chamber, Sanya tentatively picked up colour pencils and paper to draw. She looked up to check whether I was observing her. Finding me busy with the computer she felt assured and got busy with drawing some random figures, which apparently made no sense and seemingly had no connection with her present situation, ie. the conflict between her parents or anything to do with her mother's emotion of hurt, anger, or rejection.

After some time, she breached the self-imposed silence. 'Can you see what I have drawn?' she asked.

'No,' I said.

'Okay, then don't look here. I am drawing something else. I will show it to you, when it is complete,' she told me in an authoritative tone.

Sanya had drawn a grown-up girl standing by a new-born baby in a cradle. The girl was holding balloons in her hand and there were also balloons tied to the cradle.

Sanya's acceptance of the new-born as her sibling was evident. The balloons reflected her happiness and excitement at the event. Sanya was excited and even worded her desire to see her sister.

- See a professional, if need be. Take care of your mental health in order to be meaningfully available to the child.
- Moving on by the other spouse is not to belittle you. It is their way of dealing with life.
- It is the wounded ego, which causes most pain.
- Pursue your own hobbies and strengthen your own competencies rather than feeling empowered only by the child's custody.
- Let children enjoy the love and affection showered by the other; do not burden them with your own analysis. It is difficult, but possible.

Tormentor Denied Custody

HARSH'S MOTHER HAD died under mysterious circumstances. On that fateful day, his elder brother Mayank was away at tuition class while Harsh was playing a video game on the television in his parents' bedroom. Naina, Harsh's mother was ironing clothes in the same room.

The 'tring tring' of the doorbell did not reach Harsh's ear. He was deeply engrossed in killing his target. It was his father, Jignesh, he realised, when he heard him screaming at his mother. He switched off the video game as soon as he heard the commotion in the room.

'Is this the time to iron clothes?' screamed Jignesh at the top of his voice, scaring the life out of Harsh.

Naina was accustomed to such outbursts and did not react. She simply unplugged the iron and started putting the clothes away.

'Why aren't you answering?' shouted Jignesh, cheesed off by Naina's indifference. Naina kept quiet, as she knew no answer would satisfy Jignesh. His tirade would continue irrespective of her explanation.

'What do you think of yourself?' asked Jignesh and slapped Naina hard on her face.

Naina lost her balance with the impact of that tight slap and fell on the bed.

Harsh had sunk into the brown leatherette sofa in my chamber, as he recounted the sequence of events that led to his mother's death.

'Papa dragged my mother by her hair to another room, while she resisted with all her might. I also ran after my mother, but my grandmother stopped me,' narrated Harsh, surprisingly without a trace of pain on his face.

How could a child, at the tender age of nine, dispassionately narrate the torture his mother was subjected to, was beyond me.

'I heard my mother scream and call out for help. But, every time I tried to run to that room, my grandmother dissuaded me with the assurance that everything would be alright. She even served me food. That was simply to distract me, I realised later,' said Harsh and fell silent.

'I ran towards that room as soon as my grandmother went to the kitchen to fetch me a glass of water...' Harsh became quiet for a while and then continued.

'Although, I am very scared of my father, I tried pushing into that room to save my mother, but to no avail. The door was bolted from inside. I ran towards the window and saw my father beating my mother like a mad person. I froze when I saw my mother lying on the floor, left with no energy to ward off further assaults by that *shaitaan* (monster),' recalled Harsh grimly.

For the first time during that entire interaction, I saw sadness on his face. Harsh's face, in that moment, looked like the face of a mature man, weathered by the vagaries of life. His momentary silence before he continued was pregnant with grief and suppressed anger.

'Aunty, before I could think of a way to pull my mother out of the clutches of my father, I felt someone holding my collar from behind. It was my grandmother. She pulled me into the bedroom by the collar. I did not do anything, I don't know why,' said Harsh with a grimace.

'My mind had gone absolutely blank. I did not utter a single word, despite my mother being reduced to pulp. My grandmother put me to sleep along with my elder brother, Mayank, who had also returned from tuition...I don't understand why, but I could not tell Mayank about the whole thing. Mayank fell asleep as soon as he hit the bed. But, I could not sleep for a very long time and kept lying there, keeping my eyes shut, lest my grandmother scold me,' narrated Harsh.

'I do not remember when I fell asleep,' he went on.

'I did not find my mother in the house, when I woke up the next morning. Only my *bua* (paternal aunt) was there. Neither my father nor my grandparents were to be found. My bua told me that my mother had been taken to the hospital and my father and my grandparents had accompanied her,' said Harsh and fell silent.

Afraid to break the flow, I did not ask any questions. He broke his silence after a minute.

'I felt very lonely. Mayank had already left for school, when I woke up. I did not know whom to ask about my mother, although I was very worried...I knew my bua would never tell me the truth. When police visited our house in the late afternoon, I realised that something was amiss. But still no one told me anything about my mother. I simply kept quiet, waiting for Mayank to return.'

'Only when the police uncle asked me what happened to my mother, I knew something was wrong. My *nana-nani* (maternal grandparents) had come. They asked me to tell whatever I had seen, without any fear. I told them. Then nana-nani took Mayank and me to their house...Since then I have never visited my father nor has he,' told Harsh.

Jignesh had filed a petition for custody of both his sons, who were living with their maternal grandparents for more than a year since Naina passed away. This petition was hotly contested by Naina's parents.

Jignesh claimed custody, pleading that he had been framed in a case of suicide by his wife. He professed immense love for his children, alleging that they had been tutored against him by his in-laws. He also claimed that he was financially capable of taking good care of the children. Being their biological father, he could take better care of their emotional well-being as well. He said that Naina's parents were old and ailing and that they and their unmarried daughter were surviving on Naina's father's pension. He also pleaded that they could not even look after the studies of the boys.

To deflect blame for Naina's death, Jignesh had even devoted a few paragraphs of his petition to certain incidents to describe Naina as an emotionally unstable woman, who always reacted disproportionately to every situation. Jignesh had also expressed his concern about the well-being of the children once Neela, their *mausi* (mother's sister), got married stating that there wouldn't be anyone to look after the children thereafter.

Harsh and Mayank were being taken care of by Neela who during a chamber hearing shared that she had taken a vow not to marry and to bring up her sister's children as her own.

Jignesh had been in jail for about a year, before he was admitted to bail on various grounds including the one that there was no one to take care of his aged parents. Charges against Jignesh under Section 306 Indian Penal Code, 1860 for abetment of suicide by his wife had already been framed.

The boys' maternal grandparents fought tooth and nail against Jignesh's custody petition. During counselling, they made it clear that they would not allow their grandchildren to be brought up by Jignesh who had killed their daughter. They seemed really stressed out at the possibility of the custody of the children being given to their father.

In a one-to-one interaction with the boys, both of them

made it clear that they would not live with their father. Surprisingly, Mayank remained quiet, and it was the younger one, Harsh, who did most of the talking. I was really surprised by the poise with which Harsh spoke of their decision not to join their father.

'Why do you not want to live with your own father?' I asked both of them.

'He killed our mother,' both said in unison.

'How do you know that your father killed your mother?' I asked.

'Maine apni aakhon se sab kuch dekha hai...jab usne mara toh woh silent ho gayi...' emphasised Harsh. (I saw everything with my own eyes. When he hit her, she fell silent.)

Grinding his teeth, Harsh said, *'Main usse isliye baat nahi karta, na kabhi karunga...Main chup raha kyunki nahi toh mujhe bhi maar deta. Meri mummy ne kya bura kiya tha jo usne maar diya...Agar woh mujhe chedta toh main uski batti uda deta,'* continued Harsh after a pause. (That is why I don't talk to him, nor will I ever in future. I was quiet then because otherwise he would have killed me also. What wrong did my mother do that he killed her. If he had troubled me then I would have taught him a lesson.)

'Ek baar maine uda di thi uski batti,' he went silent without completing the sentence. (One time, I taught him a nice lesson.)

I also did not ask him to clarify as to how he set his father right.

*'Pichle saal seene main ghoosa mara tha usne mujhe jab main toilet ja raha tha. Woh kheench raha tha, aur main toilet ki taraf ja raha tha...*Aunty, *main roya nahi. Maine apna muh hasne wala bana liya tha,'* he continued on his own, trying to show that he was very brave. (Last year he punched me on my chest

when I was going to the toilet. He was pulling me and I was trying to drag myself to the toilet. Aunty I never cried. I kept a smile on my face all the time.)

I waited for him to share anything further.

'...*Maine sab bata diya, aur kuch nahi batana,*' he concluded, as if he had read my mind. (I have said everything. I don't want to say anything more.)

As soon as I turned my attention towards Mayank, pre-empting me, he asked, 'How can we be expected to live with the person who killed our mother.'

'I know for sure that he killed our mother,' interjected Harsh.

'*Vo agar hath me gangajal lekar bhi keh dega ki usne nahi maara, toh bhi hum uske sath nahi rahenge,*' Harsh made it clear. (Even if he swears on the water of the Ganges that he did not kill her, we will not live with him.)

As per the FIR (First Information Report), Harsh and Mayank's mother Naina had committed suicide by hanging herself from the ceiling fan with her own sari. The copy of her post-mortem report showed a number of ante-mortem injuries on Naina's body. Apparently, both the children did not know how their mother met her death. Harsh had witnessed only the beatings by Jignesh. He had seen her lying on the floor and presumed that she died because of the beatings. How deeply the trauma of losing his mother at the hands of his father must have impacted little Harsh who was witness to the beatings, I tried to assess. The only saving grace with Harsh was that he was talkative and could narrate what he felt. He was still young and innocent so he could tell the facts as facts without injecting them with his own emotions and trauma, except once or twice

'He never got me any clothes. He always made me roam around in my undergarments.'

when he emphatically said no to even seeing his father's face. I could not pierce through the calm facade put up by Mayank. I was at my wit's ends, failing to extract anything out of that twelve-year-old boy.

Jignesh had claimed custody being the biological father. In normal circumstances, the biological father has every right to meet and bond with his children. But here, the father's suitability itself was in question, in view of the nature of allegations against him, though yet to be proved. His prayer, of at least weekly visitations, was required to be tested on the touchstone of welfare of the children. Both the children were old enough to make an intelligent choice and had already expressed their revulsion at the idea.

'*Aunty aapko nahi pata, woh saara khana kha jata tha, chahe kisi aur ko mile ya na mile,*' interjected Harsh out of the blue. (Aunty, he would eat up all the food, without any consideration for others.)

'*Mujhe kabhi kapde bhi nahi dilaye, hamesha baniyan me ghumata tha...Nana hi mummy ko khane ka saaman la kar dete the... Belt se mummy ko maarta tha, pata hai aapko?*' he continued with a very grim expression on his face. (He never got me any clothes. He always made me roam around in my undergarments. Nana only got foodstuff for mom. Do you know aunty, he used to beat mom with a belt.)

'*Kuch nahi bacha ab...mummy ko mar diya isne...*' (Nothing is left now. He killed mom.)

'*Paise bhi saare chori ki hain...Raat ko jaata tha kahin...*' said Harsh after a thoughtful pause. (The money he got was stolen money. He used to go out somewhere at night.)

The law requires the court to consider the choice of the

child where he is old enough to form an intelligent preference. Harsh and Mayank were nine and twelve years old respectively and were very clear that they did not even want to meet their father. In the peculiar circumstances of this case, I was mindful of the emotional and psychological trauma they may undergo even by the suggestion of meeting their father.

The court also has to keep in mind that the child is a person within the meaning of Article 21 of the Constitution of India. Their choice would be a part of the right to life as guaranteed under Article 21.

Separate interactions in my chamber were also held with Jignesh and the maternal grandparents. No joint session could be held due to the extreme situation. Such interactions revealed the true purpose of Jignesh's custody petition. He had not sought custody out of love and affection for the boys. It was an attempt to pressurise his in-laws to succumb to a quid pro quo. That is, he would not press his claim for custody if they agreed not to pursue the charges under Section 306 Indian Penal Code against him.

It did not take me much time to understand that the custody petition was simply a camouflage for his hidden agenda of somehow wriggling out of the criminal charges against him. He wanted to create a fear in the mind of his in-laws that he could snatch the custody of the children from them. Such tactics are not new to family courts.

The court refused to give Jignesh custody of his sons, or even visitation rights.

- In extreme cases, even a biological father can be denied custody.
- As per law, character and criminal propensity of a parent is a relevant factor while deciding custody.
- Considering the age of the child and the capacity for making an intelligent choice, his preference has to be considered.

Remarriage Complexities

SAVI AND VIVEK had been married for about fifteen years and were living in America with their two children, a son and a daughter. It had been good going till Savi suspected Vivek of having an extramarital affair. The matter went to a US court; efforts at mediation failed and ultimately Savi filed a divorce petition. The petition was allowed by a Family Court Judge with the consent of both the parties. The court also passed a 'Contact and Specific Order' laying down the details of payments to be made by Vivek for the benefit of the children, towards their school fees and maintenance, etc. while allowing Vivek and his parents contact with the children, as per a detailed schedule agreed to by both the spouses.

Crisscross of litigation between Savi and Vivek before a Family Court in India, originated from Savi's petition for maintenance of children.

Sometime after the divorce, Savi shifted to India along with the children while Vivek continued to live in America. Business engagements took Vivek all over the globe. He therefore could not personally appear before the Family Court in India and was represented by an advocate. His advocate filed a detailed reply to Savi's petition, challenging it. Firstly, on the ground of jurisdiction as both the parties had submitted to the jurisdiction of a Family Court in USA and were governed by the terms and conditions of the settlement drawn before that court by mutual consent. Vivek's advocate had pleaded that for any grievance arising wherefrom, Savi was required to approach the Family Court in USA. After hearing advocates from both the sides, who raised a hot contest furthering their own stand that the Indian court does/does not have the jurisdiction to hear the matter, it was decided to hear the matter as per law[11] as the children were ordinarily residing within the jurisdiction of the court in Delhi.

Vivek alleged that Savi, in conspiracy with her parents, deprived him of meetings with his own children. She deliberately shifted the children to her parents' house, to deny him and his family members contact with them, alleged Vivek. He also said that Savi had done this, as she was extremely resentful of the fact that he had resettled in life.

Vivek had got remarried and even had a baby girl within a year of his marriage. It was Vivek's case that not only Savi, her parents also were extremely jealous that he had remarried whereas their daughter was stuck with the children and had to return to India.

'Savi's parents have been poisoning the tender minds of the children against me and my family members. They scuttled all my efforts to be in touch with the children even over the telephone,' alleged Vivek.

---

11 Section 9 of The Guardians and Wards Act, 1890

'Ma'am, whenever I call my children, Savi will either not allow me to talk to them on one pretext or the other, or will instigate the children to misbehave with me over the phone. How am I supposed to maintain my balance, when she leaves no stone unturned to keep me away from my own children, despite my supporting them in every possible way,' asked Vivek.

'I don't know why she is behaving like that after voluntarily agreeing to the terms and conditions of the divorce settlement. She wanted the divorce, I did not ask for it,' continued Vivek.

'Isn't it a gross violation of the court's order?' he asked.

Savi, on the other hand, put the entire blame on the children, saying that they did not want to meet their father.

'Ma'am you may ask the children yourself,' she suggested to the court.

It is not unusual for a spouse to feel rejected and left out once the other spouse moves on in life by getting remarried. Vivek's allegation that Savi, out of jealousy, was tutoring the children against him could not be brushed aside lightly. I decided to have an interaction with the children.

Their daughter Ishita was nearing eighteen while the son Ishaan was seven years old. A brief interaction on the very first day showed me that Ishaan simply toed Ishita's line. He was almost like a kid to her.

When I asked Ishaan if he would like to spend some time with his dad, he looked at Ishita, innocently waiting for instructions from her. Ishita looked embarrassed.

I decided to speak to the children separately, the next time.

Ishita was more an adult although she was yet to cross the legal mark of eighteen years. She appeared to have matured much before her age, perhaps having witnessed the tumultuous

Ishaan simply toed Ishita's line. He was almost like a kid to her.

relationship between her parents.

Savi had got married at the young age of twenty and had conceived Ishita within a year of her marriage. Savi and Ishita were just two decades apart and appeared to be companions more than mother and daughter. Like seasoned adults, Ishita had learnt to take sides, while pretending to be impartial. She was a child who closely identified with her mother's pain and the perceived injustice meted out to her. Children of such dysfunctional and broken families often develop a distorted vision of relationships and life.

Children do not remain untouched by the politics their parents play, firstly to survive in the relationship and thereafter to break free from the relationship. Ishita was no exception. She could not protect herself from the victimhood of her mother. Parents lose sight of their children's vulnerability while pursuing their own agenda of revenge and hatred.

'I have no issues in meeting him, after all he is my father. But he cannot force us to meet his daughter,' said Ishita sternly.

That was an indication enough that she was open to meeting her father.

'You tell me Ma'am, why should I look at his daughter's pictures? He intentionally brings her online during our video calls, knowing fully well that I hate to interact with anyone except him,' said Ishita sounding deeply hurt on being forced to be nice to Vivek's daughter.

'Do you know he has even deliberately given her a similar name? He has named her Ishy, just to irritate me and to show that I don't mean anything to him as he has my substitute now. That is why I hate Ishy,' shared Ishita.

'Can I show you a mail which he sent to our mom?' she

asked, digging into her fancy Kate Spade bag for a piece of paper. She seemed to have come prepared with all the evidence.

It was a mail from Vivek to Savi that read, 'You will have to respect and love Ishy, as your own adopted child. She cannot be abused by you and your family members. The children should be encouraged to love each other, to enjoy a healthy relationship with me and with my new family. It was you who desperately wanted a divorce, not me...You are responsible for ruining our lives...I have already paid more than I should and cannot tolerate any further insult.'

'This mail was addressed to your mom. How do you have the printout of that?' I asked her gently lest she feel offended.

'We are like friends ma'am. She shares everything with me...I am her support system,' replied Ishita with pride in her eyes.

Such explorations of the fault lines of relationships throw up interesting revelations. Unknowingly, parents involve vulnerable children in their own battles. Sometimes, such parents cross all limits and use children as their missiles.

'The separation is between you and me and not of my children from me and my new partner and child. Your request that the children meet me alone and not my daughter, who is also their sister, is unheard of amongst civilised people. Blended families are a new way of life amongst divorced couples,' read Vivek's e-mail.

That longish e-mail went on to sermonise that Savi should teach the children love and respect and stop tutoring them to misbehave with him and Ishy if she wanted the *war* to stop.

'I am warning you for the last time. Stop using the children to pursue your agenda of hatred. If you continue to keep the children away from me, I shall bequeath my entire estate to Ishy...

If the children are not mine during my lifetime; they cannot claim to be mine after my death either. It would be very painful for me to do so, but I will be compelled to take such a course in case you don't mend your ways,' threatened Vivek's e-mail.

'I am the last person to want to do that. I would rather make all my children equal beneficiaries of my wealth, in case something happens to me...Please don't push me to the wall. Do not force me to take an extreme step. I would hate doing so,' said the mail.

Ishita waited patiently while I went through that e-mail. She expected a reaction from me, as was clear from the expression on her face. I deliberately concealed my reaction. Barring a slight disappointment in her eyes, her facial expression and body language registered only satisfaction that she had been heard with patience.

'Can I show you an e-mail which Ishy sent to me calling my mother names?' asked Ishita. She pulled out another piece of paper from her bag and handed it over to me.

'Dear Didi, I love you very much...but you know the truth very well. Your mother is a BIG Liar,' read the e-mail.

I could see deep hurt in Ishita's eyes. Then she pulled out yet another e-mail from her bag. This one was again from Vivek.

'Please don't use children as bait...don't exploit any further, the large heartedness of my parents. With their growing age, they cannot bear your tantrums and hurtful tirade. Please leave them alone...You have already wasted years of our lives with your negative attitude. Please live and let me live in peace.'

'...It is high time you accepted the reality of life with an open mind...it is the choice you yourself made. I have no issue if you also move forward in life. But, for God's sake, get settled in your life and let us all be. Let the kids enjoy my company. Don't be heartless and deprive me of the joy of spending time with my children, who really love me. Please don't poison my children's impressionable minds. If you so want, I am still open to resolving any issue through mediation,' wrote Vivek.

'Ma'am, why would mom poison our minds?' asked Ishita, the moment I finished reading that e-mail. 'I am an adult. I understand everything,' she continued.

I kept silent and restrained. Soon Ishita sobered down.

By the end of the counselling session, Ishita seemed open to meeting her father with a pre-condition that Vivek would not insist that she talk to 'HIS' daughter.

At the next hearing, things took an unexpected turn. Vivek's lawyer said that Vivek was unable to visit India but he could meet the children in Canada, where they had already planned their vacations. Savi agreed but made it clear that the children would not be asked to meet Vivek's daughter. Vivek's lawyer sought an adjournment to seek instructions from him.

At the next hearing, Savi flared up like a suppressed volcano, as soon as Vivek's lawyer filed an e-mail received from him. Vivek's comment in the e-mail that he would not agree to Savi's suggestion that the children would not meet his daughter Ishy, was the obvious trigger.

'There is no way I am going to segregate my children…All of them need to love and play with each other as siblings, as children around the globe do, without any mess created by the interference of adults in children's matters…' it said.

Vivek's lawyer, after seeking instructions from him, said Vivek would meet Ishita separately, as she was the one who resisted seeing Ishy the most.

I could not really fathom why Vivek had given his daughter from the second marriage a name similar to Ishita's. Ishita was deeply hurt, as she felt that she was being substituted. Nor could I appreciate Vivek's insistence that the children interact with Ishy. He failed to see that his adamancy and insistence that the children accept Ishy as their own was only repulsing them further.

The fact that no one can be forced to love was beyond Vivek. He kept on sermonising how globally children accept their half sisters and brothers, without sparing a thought to the children's sensibilities.

Of course, children from different marriages of their parents do meet. Recently, leading dailies reported bonhomie between Jhanvi, Khushi (Boney Kapoor and Sridevi's daughters), and Anshula Kapoor (his daughter from his first wife), on the eve of a trailer launch of Jhanvi's movie *Dhadak*. But nobody knows what actually goes on behind the scenes.

Impressing upon children at such a delicate juncture to behave in a particular manner is cruel. I think one has to keep in mind the sensibilities of children. On separation of parents, children are already under stress, handling their own emotions and also providing support to the custodial parent.

It seemed to me that Savi and Vivek were embroiled in settling their own scores with each other instead of being available to their children at this crucial time. They kept trading charges, oblivious to the fact that they were adding further trauma to their already injured children.

Vivek, time and again, insisted that Savi should resolve the matter through family mediation and accept the fact that he had re-settled in life. The last arrow from his side read:

'You are a frustrated person. You and your family have nothing but war on your minds. You cannot see anything beyond money. Your love for money has ruined your life but you have not learnt any lesson. Your wait for that hidden 'golden pot' is misplaced. You have already wasted millions in courts to grab that treasure. You will continue to waste more money without any gain. You have already taken more than 90 per cent of the marital assets leaving me with nothing but debt, stress, and pain. You have also been abusing children's visitation rights to extract more funds. What sort of person are you!! You want to snatch small kids from their father. Feel free to file as many cases as you wish. Move as many courts as you like. It will only compel me to spend more money defending all such cases; leaving less and less with me for my children. There is a financial price to 'ego' in legal matters. Who should know that better than you? But you and your disgusting family are best dealt with via courts only. Yet in order to save some money for my kids, I still urge you to sit and talk through mediation.'

Vivek's mail further reminded Savi that she was sent to attend a course in 'Parenting' by the US Court, but she had not learnt anything. 'You still haven't learnt the importance of both the parents in a child's life. I beseech you to guide the children to interact with their step sibling.'

When they could not resolve the issue, Vivek issued a legal notice to Savi, pointing out:-

'...Despite repeated attempts, my efforts to resolve matters amicably through mediation have not met any success. You are not interested in any peaceful and healing process. I am now left with no choice but to serve you this legal notice.

(i) I now claim full custody of Ishaan. He should come

and live with me in the USA since you don't follow court orders and the child is suffering for paternal contact. You may have his custody/visitation during vacations or;

(ii) he may continue his remaining studies in India under 'visitation' given to you but will be in my legal custody. All school holidays shall be spent by him with me.

(iii) Their half-sister Ishy shall also have right of contact with other siblings ie. Ishita and Ishaan. Children will have to go through counselling on how to deal with a half sibling in a respectful manner. This is for betterment of all the children to learn to love. Alas! You can never understand children maintaining a perfectly normal relationship with their half siblings.

(iv) You also need to attend a course to learn how to handle a teenage child. Ishita is an example of your failure to handle her.

(v) You cannot be saved from my wrath. You yourself are responsible for this situation having scuttled every effort I made for resolution of disputes through mediation.

Vivek apparently was still not satisfied with the anger poured out by him in his legal notice. He went on to send a follow-up mail:-

'You have nothing else to occupy you the whole day except jealousy. You cannot bear that I am happy with my new life. You will always remain a miserable person like your mother.'

'I sent you my friend's pictures with his new partner and baby. He is also divorced and resettled. He picks his two kids every other week and they stay with his new partner and new baby. Those two kids from his previous marriage love to play with the baby!!! They love him like their own baby brother. My friend collects and drops his children from his home. Both respect shared custody. No drama, no *chik chik*. But you miserable woman, you will never understand this and won't let my kids interact with me and Ishy. You have your own agenda to pursue all the time. You have totally screwed up the kids' life. The only reason I kept bearing with you and didn't kick you out was that you gave birth to my two beautiful children. Now you cannot snatch my children (who were the reason of our marriage continuing this long) from me.'

'I am warning you one final time. Please stop dragging the innocent children into our issues and stop ruining their lives on account of your own frustrations.'

Vivek's frustration was writ large in his 'no holds barred' writings. He was getting totally out of control.

Psychologists say a heightened sense of drama, fear, and insecurity is natural during a calamity; they help people cope with their loss. Is that the reason why people in Family Courts enact a lot of drama? I wondered.

Various applications filed by Savi and Vivek from time to time and their acerbic contents were nothing but bitterness and frustration poured out by them, having failed marriage; and Savi not being able to handle the moving on by Vivek. They used the litigation and the court as an instrument for settling their private vengeance.

Extramarital affair of a spouse does assume importance for the purpose of determining the fitness of a parent to be the guardian of the children. But even that has to be seen in the light of all the facts and circumstances. If the husband/wife is able to demonstrate that they were unhappy in the relationship but were still taking good care of the children and shared a bond with them, they cannot be deprived of custody on this ground alone. Each case has to be decided on its own facts. Savi's main challenge to Vivek's application for modification in custody arrangement was his extramarital affair. She also claimed that once the custody matter had been decided by mutual consent, it could not be changed later. However, courts do reconsider custody arrangements when required.

As the welfare of the child is the guiding star, all orders relating to the custody of the minor are temporary orders made in the light of the existing circumstances. With changed conditions and circumstances, including the passage of time, the Court can vary such orders if such variation is considered to be in the interest and welfare of the wards.

As per law, orders relating to custody of wards even when based on consent are liable to be varied by the Court, if the welfare of the wards demands it. Therefore, Vivek's fitness had to be considered, determined, and weighed predominantly in terms of the welfare of the minor children.

The family is the heart of our society, and for the balanced and healthy growth of children, it is highly desirable that they get their due share of affection and care from both the parents in their normal parental home. But situations like these call for a delicate balancing act so that children get love and care from both the parents and respective family members, unaffected by the relational turmoil of their parents.

I sincerely hoped that Savi and Vivek would, for the sake of their offspring, forget the past and provide their children a happy and joyous time with both the parents. They were educated and cultured and came from highly respectable families, but apparently did not realise that it was in the larger interest of the health, normal growth, and development of their children that they cooperate and work harmoniously.

Fortunately, like happy endings in Bollywood movies, with little hiccups, Ishita, by the end of the counselling sessions, agreed to meet her father. 'I will do as *didi* says,' said Ishaan, in a separate session, like a small obedient brother.

Pleasantly, Vivek agreed not to insist that the two meet their step-sibling during this visit.

Such happy endings are rare and deeply satisfying.

When 'IN' the situation, people generally lose all objectivity. It becomes difficult for them to get out of the web of their own emotional hurt. This emotional mishmash blinds them to the emotions of the other. This case certainly was a marvel achieved through the active assistance of advocates from both the sides.

Lawyers can play a very meaningful role in assisting the court and the involved spouses and children to arrive at a solution, suitable to all.

- Hurt and jealousy are best avoided in case the spouse moves on after divorce and gets remarried.
- After break-up, take some 'me time' to reflect and make a conscious effort to wipe clean the old relationship and its residue.
- After legal break-up, snap emotional ties and cut the cord.
- Unknowingly parents involve vulnerable children

in their own battles and even use them as their missiles, which is surely avoidable.

- No doubt, insulating children from the emotional upheaval of parents may not be possible, but an effort can be made to lessen its impact on them, by not involving them too much or manipulating them for your own agenda of revenge and hatred.
- Children's sensibilities need to be borne in mind. Insistence on meeting as per your own plans can alienate children further.
- Advocates can play a positive role in assisting the court, the spouses, and children to find options and solutions.

Mr Right

MY CULTIVATED PATIENCE snaps at times when civilised-looking spouses get too vicious and lock horns. Their rhetoric sometimes gives the sense that they are eternally entangled... God knows for how many lifetimes.

Rohan's case was a little different. Neeta, his estranged wife, was petite, soft-spoken, demure, and generally did not react to his vitriolic outbursts. She simply narrated her version, seemingly unaffected by all the allegations levelled against her by Rohan.

Rohan and Neeta had been living separately for more than six years. Rohan had filed a petition for the custody of their daughter, Vidisha, who had been living with Neeta since she was a baby. Neeta had given birth to Vidisha a few months after she shifted to her parents' house.

Neeta had not filed for divorce so far, although she was contemplating the move. She had filed a complaint with the Crime Against Women Cell alleging cruelty by Rohan and his family. Her case was that there were subtle demands for dowry,

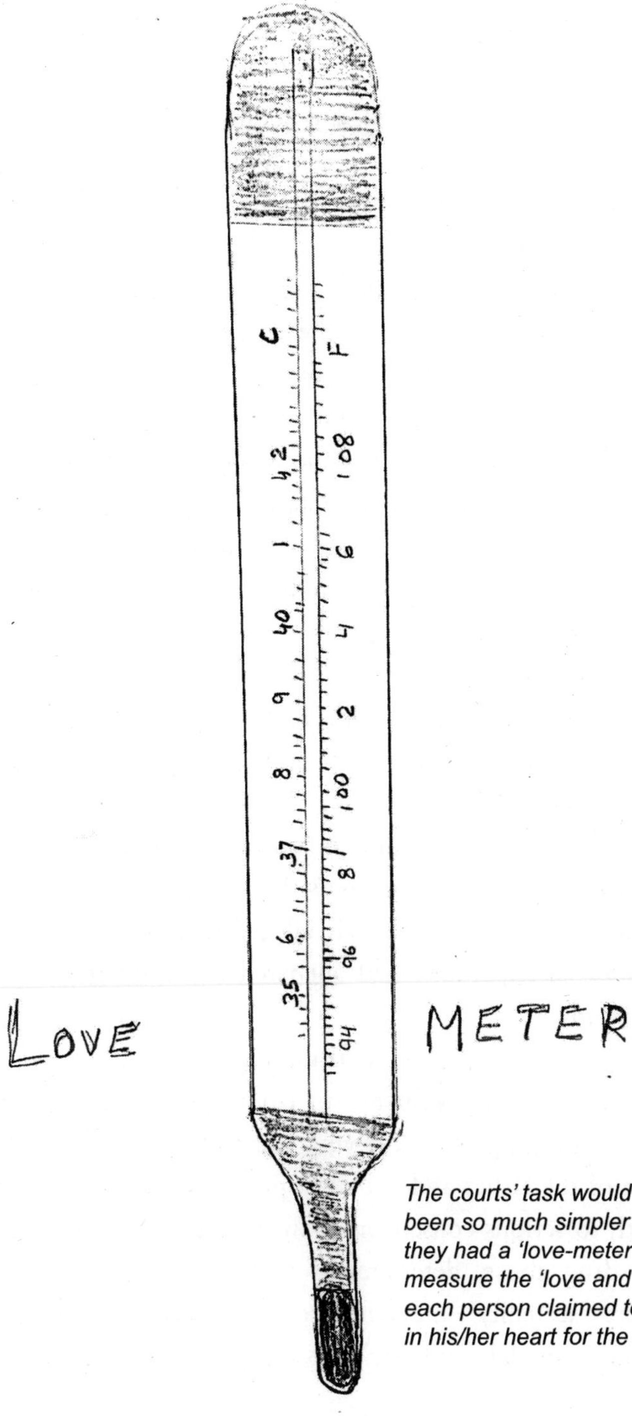

The courts' task would have been so much simpler if they had a 'love-meter' to measure the 'love and care' each person claimed to have in his/her heart for the child.

and the birth of a daughter added to her miseries. Her daughter was obliquely referred to as a burden and rejected outright. Rohan never made an effort to take them back to his home.

Rohan simply denied all these allegations. He said he wanted custody as he loved his daughter immensely and was better equipped financially and otherwise to take care of her.

'I work from home and therefore can be more available to Vidisha. My mother and grandmother are also very attached to her. Even Vidisha loves them a lot and wishes to spend time with them,' Rohan stated in his petition, to make his claim weighty.

I wish courts had a 'love-meter' to measure the 'love and care' each person claimed to have in his/her heart for the child. The courts' task would have been so much simpler.

Generally, spouses do not stop with claims that their company is better for the child. The emphasis invariably is more on why it is not good for the child to stay with the other spouse. Rohan was no exception. He alleged that Neeta had left her matrimonial home due to constant interference of her parents and other family members. Her brother and his wife had undue influence over her. He alleged that Neeta's brother and *bhabhi* (sister-in-law) had alienated the child from him and his family.

He alleged in his custody petition that:

'Neeta, under the influence of her brother and sister-in-law, is not grasping that depriving the child of the love and affection of the father and denial of proper access to him will give birth to serious consequences in the later life of Vidisha, such as drug abuse, deteriorating educational achievement, premature sexuality, mental/personality disorder, chronic depression, suicidal tendency, out-of-wedlock birth, often a major force behind serious crimes. In our Indian society and in particular Hindu society, anybody seeking matrimonial alliance will certainly give due importance to the girl's relationship with her father and a living father's absence will surely invite doubts and may draw remarks too.'

Some of these claims were hilarious. How would the child's alienation lead to 'premature sexuality' or for that matter 'out-of-wedlock birth,' remained a mystery to me. It seemed to me that these assertions were the outcome of the fertile imagination of Rohan's advocate. Spouses can do themselves a favour by going through the petition drafted by their advocates before signing the same.

Rohan also claimed in his petition that he was very liberal in spending money on toys, books, educational aids, food items, etc. for the child and would continue to do so irrespective of his relationship with Neeta. Rohan said he would ensure that Vidisha took part in extracurricular activities such as reading, writing, painting, dancing, etc. to make her personality *vibrant*. Rohan wished to take the child on vacations during school breaks to 'expand Vidisha's knowledge base' and also to bond closely with her so that she always had a feeling of security and the confidence of having a caring and loving father and grandmother.

It was interesting that Rohan wanted to do everything for Vidisha in the *future*—once her custody was handed over to him. He was least concerned with what was happening to Vidisha currently due to his tug of war with his wife. He was oblivious to the fact that his telling the child that he was a great father and putting down her mother was impacting the child in the *present* moment.

How could parents who claimed that they were ready to

do anything for the child, create such a hostile atmosphere, depriving the child of happiness at the present moment!

Rohan claimed that he was more educated than Neeta. He even tried to show Neeta in a poor light by pleading that she could not pronounce many English words properly, whereas he was proficient in the language and could take good care of Vidisha's education. As if the entire education of the child hinged on the English language!

Neeta did not speak much during court proceedings. In the counselling session, she said that she had no objection to Rohan meeting Vidisha once or twice a month. But she had reservations about giving him overnight custody as she feared that Rohan and his parents may pollute the child's mind. She shared some of her past experiences.

Interaction with six-year-old Vidisha left me deeply concerned about her well-being. Vidisha seemed to be under immense pressure. It was a herculean task to make her speak. The initial sessions with her were quite frustrating. Over a period of time, she started responding in monosyllables.

Spouses have different ways of taking revenge on each other. Rohan drew sadistic pleasure in tormenting Neeta by filing one application after the other, insisting many a time on her personal presence on the plea that he sincerely wanted to explore the possibility of a settlement. He knew very well that every personal appearance would cost Neeta one leave from her job. Such applications, of course, met the fate they needed to meet. But they did add to Neeta's anxiety.

Instead of accepting the fact that they were not meant for each other and were unable to live together, Rohan kept on adding to the web of litigation. Rather than working on providing for Vidisha, whom he claimed to love so much, knowingly or unknowingly, Rohan kept on creating traumatic situations for her.

I wished with all my heart that, for the child's sake, Rohan and Neeta could work out a way of sharing togetherness with the child, even if they carried grudges against each other.

This case was a shade easier to deal with, as only one spouse, ie. Rohan, needed to be handled dexterously. However, Rohan's persona itself was so aggressive that his presence alone triggered the turbulent energy in the courtroom full of aggrieved and victim spouses. Handling Vidisha also was a test of patience and communication skills. She hardly uttered a word during interaction.

After much deliberation and counselling, Rohan was allowed visitation rights for about two hours once in a fortnight. The meeting was to take place in the children's room in the Family Court Complex, taking into account the utter distrust between the parents and the vulnerability of the young child.

But, it turned out that even the meetings in the children's room were stressful for the child, the parents, and even for the court. Rohan and Neeta would argue at every meeting. Neeta would always insist that she be allowed to sit inside the children's room while Rohan met Vidisha. Rohan's plea would be that Neeta influenced Vidisha; in her presence, Vidisha hesitated in interacting with him.

After much cajoling and coaxing, finally it was agreed that Rohan would meet Vidisha in the presence of the counsellor. But to my dismay even that did not work. On more than one occasion, Neeta alleged that the counsellor pulled Vidisha inside when she refused to enter the children's room. Much ruckus was created and both of them levelled allegations against each other and insisted on calling for CCTV recordings. Finding no other way, I was compelled to ask Rohan to meet the child at 5 pm, in my chamber, in my presence, though I felt that even my presence hindered a free flow of energy between the father and daughter. Rohan made Vidisha sit on his lap and gave her his laptop to play some games. For the first time, I saw a faint smile cross Vidisha's lips but the two hardly spoke to each other. On the next date, Neeta did not bring Vidisha which led to bitter arguments between the two. Rohan claimed that whenever there was some progress in the bonding between him and Vidisha, Neeta found a way to break the continuity and did not allow the bond to develop.

'Vidisha was very upset after meeting Rohan, the last time; so much so that she had to skip school. I had to take Vidisha to a psychiatrist,' claimed Neeta.

'With great difficulty, Vidisha is now reverting back to normal. I cannot allow her to undergo the same turmoil all over again,' declared Neeta in no uncertain terms.

'He only thinks about himself. Had he been concerned about her well-being, he would not have insisted upon meeting Vidisha today, after knowing that she had to skip school because of vomiting and headache due to emotional turmoil at the previous meeting,' commented Neeta.

Lo! Neeta had hardly finished when Rohan erupted like a volcano, 'All this is bullshit. This is a new drama to keep me away from my own daughter.'

Neeta seemed well prepared today. She took out a medical report from her bag and handed it over to the court.

Rohan demanded a copy of the report but Neeta said she

did not have one. They argued while I went through the report.

Courts cannot brush aside medical reports but they do have to have an independent assessment of the situation. It was a tough call.

The psychiatrist's report read:

> 'Ms Vidisha, aged six and half years, was assessed by me. The child was brought to the clinic with complaints of stomach ache, nausea, etc. which reportedly happen only on certain specific days of the month. The child's maternal grandfather, mother, and child herself were interviewed in detail. They were, thus, the chief informants.
>
> 'Her adjustment at home and social domain functioning at home is also reported normal. The child's parents got separated before the child's birth and the child has been brought up and taken care of by the mother and maternal grandparents since her birth. The child is a single child, staying with her mother at her maternal grandparents' place since her birth. There is reportedly a litigation going on between the child's parents.
>
> 'Vidisha, a student of class II, is an active, alert, and healthy child who follows directions. She has diverse interests and achievements in creative domains like dance, music, art, etc. and has adequate peer functioning, school attendance, and school adjustment as evident from her school report cards.
>
> 'Overall the child seemed to be bright, intelligent, and emotionally sensitive.
>
> 'The child has been recurrently crying and complaining of stomach ache, nausea, distress, fatigue, and suffering from disturbed sleep around the time when the visitation days (days when the child has to meet the father in the court) are scheduled in the month.
>
> 'Recently, the child complained of severe stomach ache in the morning, had episodes of crying, was

> excessively stressed to the extent that she had a minor episode of left nasal bleeding. The child was taken to a medical practitioner who did not find any organic physical illness and advised not to lay any kind of stress on the child in addition to suggesting pharmacological intervention.'
>
> The psychiatrist further observed that, 'on detailed assessment, the most probable precipitating factor could be that the child had to meet the father in the court that day. The child further revealed that she is being subjected to these meetings against her wishes and that she is also physically handled as she says, *Mujhe godi mein bethate hai papa* (Papa makes me sit on his lap), indicating the visitations to be a major area and source of stress, resentment, and helplessness in the child.'
>
> 'The mother also reported similar physical complaints of stomach ache, body aches, and distress of the child earlier too, especially when meetings of the child with the father were held without the mother's presence in the meeting room.
>
> 'In sessions taken individually with the child, the child evaded all talk about the father. She did not express any desire to meet the father and started crying. Her behaviour revealed negative and unpleasant nature of interaction between the father and the child during the visitations.'

This seemed somewhat contrary to what had happened during the meeting between father and daughter in my chamber, unless the child could fake the smile on her face.

The psychiatrist's report concluded:

> 'A detailed analysis of the child was done to ascertain and establish a correlation between the psychological factors and the child's somatic complaints. Since, the child's entire history is normal, it may be said that the pain and other somatic problems that the child is experiencing

seem to be arising out of intense and precipitating stress that the child is experiencing during the visitations.'

It becomes quite a task for the court to arrive at its own conclusion after having before it such findings. However, the possibility of such reports being influenced can also not be ruled out.

The visitations were perforce discontinued, Vidisha being unwell.

When the child is traumatised due to meeting with a parent, there is no other option but to discontinue such meetings. Non-availability of services of experts/psychologists/psychiatrists to Family Courts is deeply felt in such situations. Reference then needs to be made to psychiatrists/child psychologists at a government hospital and such an assessment is a long-drawn process requiring several sittings with the child.

Vidisha was referred to a child psychiatrist at AIIMS (All India Institute of Medical Sciences).

- More often than not parents promise to do various things for the child in future, when the custody is handed over to them. But in the present, while custody is with the other, they avoid making a bare minimum contribution towards the child's expenses.
- A psychologist's report produced by the custodial parent based on a parent/grandparents' feedback runs the risk of being tainted. Instead of any assistance, it may sometimes complicate the issues.
- Non-availability of such expert help to Family Courts is a constraint.

The Technology Trap

LATA HAD A complaint that Akshit, her only son was always glued to the screen and did not step out of the house at all.

'Remove him from one screen and you will find him before another one. I am now tired of it,' said Lata.

'I seem like a villain in his life. Whereas his father Animesh, who gets his custody for three hours in a week, takes him out and buys him the choicest of things. He has bought him yet another gadget, adding to my problems,' complained Lata.

That was not the only grievance Lata had.

'Akshit does not stop singing his father's praises. Whenever I say something to him, he simply dismisses me,' was her other refrain.

'"Papa is very good. He takes me around to malls, buys me chocolates and gifts. You only scold me and ask me to study all the time or command me to do this or that," he says,' shared Lata, expecting a quick-fix solution from me.

Lata was not wrong in worrying about Akshit's screen fixation. It is well known now that too much screen time takes a toll on children's health.

The impact of too much exposure to technology on a child's psyche can be gauged from the results of yet another study. Recently, a national daily reported that a study revealed that one of the factors for rise in suicide rates among teenagers between 2010 and 2015 could be the rising use of social media. Cyber bullying and social media posts depicting perfect lives of others may be taking a toll on the mental health of teenagers. One of the youngsters shared that after hours of scrolling through Instagram feeds, he felt worse about himself on finding that none of his posts had been liked and he felt left out.

'Excessive time on electronic devices is linked to a higher risk of depression and suicide among teenagers, especially girls,' reported a study—co-authored by Dr Thomas Joiner—Florida State University's 'Robert O Lawton Distinguished Professor of Psychology'—published in the journal *Clinical Psychological Science.*

Rujuta Diwekar, a Mumbai based nutritionist, recently shared with a leading daily[12] that 'a positive correlation has been found between screen time, consumption of sugar-sweetened beverages (packaged juices, colas, etc.), and anthropometry (incidences of overweight and obese kids) across the European Union region. One of the reasons for this is the blurred lines between entertainment and advertisements that our kids consume on the gadgets.'

Rujuta says that 'a recent study has also shown that the incidence of non-alcoholic fatty liver disease (NAFLD), a lifestyle disease in Indian kids, is rising. It could lead to liver damage similar to that seen in alcoholics. The way out is to

12 The Times Of India, 28 May 2018

Study shows that there is a correlation between screen time, consumptionn of sweetened beverages, and obesity among children.

reduce junk food, especially that loaded with sugar, and to exercise. But for that we would have to understand the factors which drive kids to gadgets and how gadgets influence both consumption of junk food and sedentary behaviour.' She made the point that 'a lot of school work is now done on laptops and tablets which makes it very important that parents lay down strict rules for screen time—be it gaming, social media, or anything else. This is easier said than done and we often tend to give in to pester power, a child's ability to demand the gadget and throw a tantrum until the demand is met.' She also makes the point that there is no other option than to say NO to kids for gadgets and the resulting junk food demand, in order to protect them from cardio-metabolic risks in the future.

We cannot deny that in their own busyness, parents have found an easy way to keep children engaged and not to bother them by complaining of boredom.

Rujuta points out, that researchers have shown, that boredom is critical for a child and, in fact, essential for creativity to blossom.

Such cases are quite common, where non-custodial parents shower the child with choicest of gadgets during their visitation time. Through these gadgets, such parents try to prove their love and affection to their children in the limited time slot available to them.

The bizarre impact of getting hooked on social media on young children again came to the fore very recently, when a national daily[13] reported that a school girl, who went missing from Pantnagar in Uttarakhand on 1 July 2019, allegedly inspired by the mobile game *Taxi Driver 2*, returned home after roaming around several cities for a fortnight.

Her 'adventure' ended in Delhi, when a police patrol spotted her loitering in Kamla Market. According to police, the girl was hooked on *Taxi Driver 2*—a South Korean 3D mobile driving game in which the players get behind the wheels of a taxi and race their way, with their clients, through a huge metropolis—ever since she started playing it on her mother's phone.

Since 1 July, when she left Pantnagar with Rupees 14,000 in her pocket, she had travelled to Rishikesh, Haridwar, Udaipur, Jaipur, Ahmedabad, and even Pune. Police said the girl would pick random destinations and was on the move 24X7, much like the cabbies in *Taxi Driver 2*. She would travel by night and explore the cities during the day.

A friend of the girl shared that she was an introvert and spent much of her time playing the video game.

---

13 Times City, The Times of India, Delhi dated 22 July 2019

'Introvert teenagers must be given attention by the parents. They should be given more exposure to the real world than the virtual world,' says Dr Nimesh Desai, Director, Institute of Human Behaviour and Allied Sciences.

How to expect maturity from warring spouses is a moot question. Co-operation by both parents; and putting their heads together to draw a schedule of the child's activities and discuss the things they should have, would go a long way in resolving these issues.

- In their own busyness, parents have found an easy way to keep children engaged, that is, provide them with gadgets.
- Gadgets provided to children to keep them happy may not only lead to obesity but also to various behavioural issues.
- Don't give in to pester power.
- Next time, don't succumb to children's complaint of boredom; boredom is critical for creativity to blossom.
- Showering children with choicest gifts/gadgets to win them over is surely avoidable.
- Cooperation from both the sides is called for, keeping aside personal grudges.

A Vast Canvas

EIGHT-YEAR-OLD Nithya stayed with her mother Vaishali in Delhi while her father Anurag stayed in Cape Town, South Africa. Anurag visited them almost every month. Anurag's parents often accompanied him when he came to visit Nithya and Vaishali in India.

Anurag was a tall suave man with hooded eyes. His behaviour had western overtones. He would present his submissions in a very gentlemanlike manner, unlike the generally loud and 'into your face' Indian spouses.

Vaishali, who was slim and very fair, was a woman of few words. Her facial contours always presented a very melancholic expression. I do not remember ever having seen a smile on her face.

Vaishali, who lived in Delhi and worked with a multinational company at Gurugram, had taken an informed decision to marry Anurag, who belonged to an established business family and lived with his extended family in Cape Town.

'Prior to marriage, Vaishali had happily agreed to quit her job and settle in Cape Town. However, soon after the wedding, she started blaming me for ruining her life and career,' said Anurag.

'Ma'am, my family and I wanted the child to be born in Cape Town and Vaishali was registered with a leading hospital with modern infrastructure, but she insisted on having the delivery in India and did not pay any heed to my entreaties,' he further shared.

'I had no other option but to allow her to travel to India in the advanced stage of her pregnancy. Although it was agreed that she would be back one and a half months after her delivery, she stayed put in India for about a year post delivery. No amount of persuasion worked with her,' he complained.

During this period, Anurag regularly visited Nithya and Vaishali and continued to provide for them financially.

'I was thrilled to have Vaishali and Nithya at Cape Town, about thirteen months after Nithya's birth. Her arrival was hugely celebrated by my parents and the entire extended family. A lavish party was thrown to welcome the arrival of Nithya into our family. But our excitement was short-lived, as Vaishali, a week after her arrival, announced that she wished to settle in India and raise the child there.'

'I was crestfallen and my mind went totally blank. I was unable to even respond to the announcement made by Vaishali, so heartlessly, without caring for my feelings or those of my parents. I shuddered at the thought of my parent's reaction, if they came to know about Vaishali's decision. I hoped against hope that Vaishali would change her mind, once she spent more time with all of us and saw Nithya being showered with so much of love and affection,' said Anurag with melancholy.

'Vaishali would stay aloof all the time. Initially I tried to ignore, hoping that it was a passing phase. But I was proved wrong when Vaishali started picking quarrels over petty things not only with me, but also with my parents. Her behaviour started turning from bad to worse. She wouldn't show a moment's hesitation in yelling at me, even in front of the staff at home,' continued Anurag.

Suddenly, Anurag fell silent, as if delving deep into his past to gather all the pain and hurt, he had hidden in the crevices of his being. Seeing me waiting for him to finish, Anurag got a little embarrassed. 'Sorry Ma'am, I just lapsed into my past,' he said apologising profusely.

During the individual counselling session, Anurag continued his share, 'I agreed to Vaishali's short visit to India thinking that she would have a break and some "me time" to reflect. I was kind of sure that she would realise what the child would be missing in India. Vaishali's family comprised only her father. Her mother had died of a dreaded disease when Vaishali was hardly nine years of age. She was brought up by her father single-handedly. Her brother, Aniket, also hardly had any interaction with Vaishali and their father, as he was married and settled in Germany.'

'I was totally heartbroken when, after leaving for India, Vaishali refused to return. However, my visits to India continued regularly, every month. In my interaction with her, I felt that Vaishali had not completely ruled out the option of returning. I was keeping my fingers crossed.'

'But again I was proved wrong when during one of my visits, Vaishali announced that she did not wish to return to Cape Town ever, and was absolutely clear that she wanted to settle in India, with the child…' Anurag continued after a short pause exhaling deeply, 'However, a month later, due to the persuasion and intervention of family members, Vaishali agreed to return.'

'Ma'am things were going just fine till one morning when Vaishali expressed a desire to visit her father in Delhi on her mother's death anniversary. I readily agreed and booked our tickets to India. After staying with them for about a week, I returned to Cape Town. Vaishali however stayed back on the pretext of wanting to spend some more time with her father.

But, it came as a shock to me when instead of returning to Cape Town, Vaishali got herself enrolled for some course in India. I was very upset when I came to know that Vaishali had even started looking for a boarding school for Nithya. I really wanted to keep Nithya close to me. When my entire family and I were available for taking care of her, there was no need for sending Nithya to a boarding school. Vaishali started isolating Nithya from all of us. I did not allow that to happen and continued to visit Nithya regularly. Even my parents visited India off and on, to keep in touch with Nithya. With resistance from our side, Nithya was put in a regular school in Delhi, which was a great relief to me and my parents, though the school was not very good.'

Anurag had filed a petition under Section 7 of Guardianship & Wards Act for declaring him the legal guardian; and also for grant of permanent custody of Nithya to him. He had also prayed that pending final disposal of the said petition, he be allowed to take minor Nithya to their matrimonial home at Cape Town. He had pleaded that Nithya was of a very tender age and required to be raised at a place, which afforded her a better life and greater future prospects.

Anurag in his petition went on to describe how he would be able to provide a better environment and wherewithal for the all-round development of Nithya.

'My family is in a superior financial position. Our house is bigger, better, and furnished with all the utilities to render all sorts of comforts to Nithya in comparison to the accommodation available with Vaishali and her father. They live in a small house on the first floor in Greater Kailash. The house does not have any garden or open space or play area for Nithya. They cannot offer the lifestyle and luxury, which we are in a position to give her,' Anurag had mentioned, in his petition.

To convince the court that he would prove to be a better parent, Anurag had further mentioned, 'Notwithstanding the luxuries available at the disposal of my family, I have been brought up in such a manner that I have grown up to be a modest person. I want to bring up my daughter in a similar fashion, so that she learns to respect elders, behaves well, has a firm grounding, and is well educated.'

Anurag further elaborated in his petition, how Nithya received/would receive love and affection and the best of environment, if her custody was given to him. He stated, 'I will make sure that Nithya's needs are completely taken care of at home. Earlier also, I made sure that Nithya stuck to a proper routine, so that she grew up as a disciplined girl. Nithya's other needs with respect to education and sports were also being taken care of, so that she received a wholesome upbringing for an all-round development of her personality. I have already shortlisted the best schools in Cape Town for Nithya's education. She is very fond of horses and taking the same into consideration, I even got her a horse as a pet besides other pets, which include dogs, rabbits, ducks, and fish; all these pets are well accommodated in our large estate.'

In his petition, Anurag had further pleaded that by keeping

In Cape Town, Nithya would grow up in a vast estate amidst nature.

Nithya in India and denying her custody to him, Vaishali was also keeping her away from the culture and traditions of her father, which he felt she should also be exposed to.

'Even in Cape Town, Vaishali hardly took any interest in Nithya's upbringing. She was always busy taking care of her family litigation in India; and had even been regularly flying to India to take care of the same,' lamented Anurag.

'Not only that, Vaishali even took Nithya along with her during such visits. Consequently, I was compelled to regularly fly to India to see and take care of Vaishali and Nithya,' added Anurag.

In his petition, Anurag had given a long list of the dates when he visited India. He claimed that the same showed his genuine concern for Nithya's welfare.

There was actually no doubt, that the mild-mannered Anurag was very fond of his daughter and was always seen deeply engaged with her.

Another plea which was taken in his petition by Anurag was that, 'Vaishali is not a fit person to take the responsibility of Nithya. She is always occupied with her work and there is no one in her family to meaningfully interact with Nithya and take care of her. She has no other family except her old and ailing father, who is not in a state to take care of Nithya as he himself is dependent upon others to take care of him.'

Anurag also pleaded that Nithya was forced to live an isolated life in Delhi. At Vaishali's place, Nithya had no other children to play with. Vaishali herself, being a recluse, did not have many friends.

'Recently I noticed certain changes in Nithya. She is no more her old energetic and vibrant self. I am really concerned. I can sense that Nithya misses me and her paternal grandparents. She feels pulled apart from the extended family, her favourite home, and the activities which were available to her at Cape Town,' Anurag further averred.

Vaishali opposed Anurag's petition but she did not dispute the financial well-being of Anurag, and the love and affection showered by him and his family members on Nithya. She did not even contest the fact that Anurag and his family lived in a sprawling estate and had a flourishing business in Cape Town.

Vaishali did not dispute that her family consisted of her and her ailing and aged father. Though, she stated that she was capable of providing good care and upbringing to Nithya.

'Ma'am, there are examples galore of single mothers having raised wonderful human beings,' Vaishali said in an attempt to convince me in one of the counselling sessions.

'I have no issue in Nithya meeting her father at regular intervals. I have never even opposed her paternal grandparents meeting her, but I cannot live without her,' said Vaishali, with a lump in her throat.

'Ma'am I am taking every possible care of Nithya and trying to provide her the best of facilities. I have even kept a tutor for taking care of her studies and her homework,' she added to bring home her point.

'If Nithya's custody is given to me, my entire family and I will always be available to Nithya,' reiterated Anurag.

'It would be better for Nithya's upbringing, as both her paternal grandparents are fit; and are able to devote all their time to their grand-daughter,' Anurag added for emphasis.

Children bloom into beautiful human beings when surrounded by the love of parents, grandparents, uncles, aunts, brothers and sisters, cousins, etc. Benefits of having grandmothers around are not unknown. Even young ones of killer whales benefit from the presence of grandmothers, suggests a new study.

In evolutionary biology, scientists call this the 'grandmother effect,' and have hypothesised that this is one of the reasons humans live so long.

Humans know the benefits of having a grandmother close by; the extra help with childcare, the reassuring advice borne from years of experience.

A new study published in the 'Proceedings of the National Academy of Sciences', of United States of America found that grandmother killer whales helped improve their grandcalves' chances of survival, particularly when food was scarce.

'They are less likely to die when she's alive than in the years following her death,' said Stuart Nattrass, the study's lead author.[14]

---

14 Article by Michael Levenson in Times Trends, The Times of India, 12 December 2019

Anurag also put across another point for Nithya's custody. 'I was exposing Nithya to various languages, including English, Hindi, and Malayalam, which I believe is essential for Nithya. Cape Town has better educational and career prospects for Nithya in comparison to India.'

Undoubtedly, Anurag and his family were very well off and his parents were very attached to Nithya. Anurag's family had business interests spread across Cape Town, South Africa, and other parts of the world. Nithya was the first grandchild in their family and was the prospective heir of the business.

'Ma'am, to succeed the business, it is necessary for Nithya to be exposed to the business environment and lifestyle at this age so that she does not face any problems in future...Nithya may lose out on learning business skills in case the custody is not given to me,' claimed Anurag.

Pleasantly, unlike other spouses, Anurag exercised restraint and did not list the negatives of Vaishali except stating that Vaishali was a very emotional and self-centred person; she hardly had any emotional bonding with people.

'Vaishali is emotionally unstable. There have been occasions when she did things that no normal person could or would do,' Anurag had mentioned without giving any further details.

'She also gets very aggressive sometimes...On one occasion, in a party, Vaishali hit me hard and started shouting at me for reasons best known to her...' Anurag said in one of the counselling sessions. He did not elaborate on the incident any further, though I waited for a while.

'Ma'am, there have been occasions when she attacked me unprovoked and scratched me all over with her sharp nails, leaving me in pain for weeks together. Not only this, on one occasion Vaishali spat on my face on a trivial matter. It can be very unsafe to keep Nithya in her custody,' said Anurag with a grimace, as though reliving the pain.

In yet another counselling session, Anurag confided that Vaishali even had suicidal tendencies and made a point that she was not only a threat to herself, but to Nithya also.

'Ma'am, I have not mentioned in my petition and I am sharing this in confidence. You can confirm it with Vaishali also. On one occasion, Vaishali became very angry with Nithya; and threatened to kill her in a fit of rage. She also told the poor child that she would kill herself also,' shared Anurag.

Vaishali did not refute the accusation of the suicide attempt made by her.

Anurag added that Vaishali's volatile behaviour could also be seen from the fact that she regularly sacked and changed nannies until hiring agencies got fed up of dealing with her. Frequent change of nannies had also been very unsettling for Nithya. By the time Nithya settled with one nanny, she was fired. Anurag also pointed out that while at Cape Town, Vaishali hardly devoted any time to Nithya. She spent hours talking on the phone, having long discussions with her lawyer/father/others, about various litigations, she/her family was involved in.

Anurag had yet another 'crucial' point to make. Vaishali would not be a good mother to Nithya; Vaishali herself had told his cousin in Cape Town that she was not able to cope with Nithya's upbringing and was finding it hard to manage her.

'Vaishali let the maid servants take care of almost every need of the child and hardly involved herself with Nithya. Vaishali also did not have any sense of balance. She made Nithya wear multiple layers of clothes even when it was hot, not caring that it was making the child uncomfortable,' said Anurag.

Another grievance of Anurag was that, 'Vaishali could not deal with the smallest health issues of Nithya and would always call my mother for help...She would administer allopathic medicines to Nithya at the drop of a hat.'

'Ma'am, Vaishali is obsessed with fair skin and puts unnecessary restrictions on Nithya if she plays outside for long. She does not allow Nithya to play on the beach lest she get tanned...You only tell me Ma'am, can this be a reason for not allowing the child to play in nature and bloom,' asked Anurag.

For the court, it was a very delicate situation. Nithya was only seven years old and a mother's company was crucial at this stage. At the same time, it was apparent that Vaishali was not equipped to take as much care and to provide wherewithal for the all-round development of Nithya which Anurag was capable of. Anurag not only had an extended family to take care of the emotional and other needs of Nithya, but was also capable of providing various facilities for her overall growth. He could arrange an array of activities for Nithya, ranging from horse riding to learning music. He could provide her an excellent upbringing amidst nature, as he lived in a huge estate. Nithya also had her cousin brothers and sisters to play with at Cape Town.

At Cape Town, Nithya had a huge canvas to paint her life on, whereas in India with Vaishali, Nithya had none of this. Though, Nithya was going to a good school in Delhi, it was not the best. Also, she had no company of her age, in Delhi. Rather, she only had her maternal grandfather for company during the day when her mother Vaishali was away at work. It

Nithya
Tree

was a fact that due to busyness of Vaishali, a tutor took care of Nithya's homework and studies. Vaishali had no time, even if she wanted to, to take charge of Nithya's studies.

On one occasion, during a chamber meeting, Nithya drew a picture of a tree on a piece of paper but spelt it incorrectly as 'trea'. Though both parents were convent educated and Nithya was even being tutored, still she could not spell that simple word correctly. It may not be a big deal, but keeping in mind Nithya's background and the fact that she was studying in class three, it did give a sense that Vaishali was not able to devote necessary attention towards Nithya. It also lent some credence to the point Anurag was making.

During my interactions with Nithya, I found her to be very hesitant. She was a very sweet child but had not bloomed to her full potential which actually worried me.

From various interactions with Vaishali, I could sense that she was a little temperamental and needed emotional support herself.

It was a pretty tough call to balance all the factors for deciding the custody case. On one hand was available, a vast canvas of life to spread the chosen colours on. On the other hand was the constricted life of a metro with a mother, who had many issues ranging from her own emotional baggage of the childhood trauma of losing her mother to a dreaded disease to taking care of an ailing father to a lot of hurt and mistrust, she had inherited from her family. Then there was also the fact that her family was entangled in a criss-cross of litigations amongst themselves.

On her father's side, Nithya had a very happy, well-knit large extended family with every possible facility, one could dream of.

It is said that we create our own destiny by the choices we

make. But can young Nithya exercise the right to choose between the two worlds? Each world was pulling her towards itself.

It was a tough call even for the court, to choose on behalf of Nithya, being her *parens patriae*.

Fortunately, with the intervention of the court and good offices of advocates of both sides, they agreed not to insist on handing over Nithya's custody to Anurag. Both agreed to share the custody. It was agreed that Nithya would spend vacations with Anurag at Cape Town, and Anurag and his parents would also visit Nithya at Delhi for two days in a month. During these two-day visits, Anurag would have overnight custody of Nithya.

This arrangement worked well for the interregnum pending disposal of the custody petition.

- Before marrying a person settled abroad, take your time and weigh all the pros and cons lest you face adjustment issues post-marriage.
- It is better to share with your spouse before getting into marital alliance, your responsibilities toward your parental family, which would need your time and attention, post marriage
- It is okay to part with the child's custody, if you realise that you cannot be available to the child as much as the other can—of course, after ensuring that you have adequate access to the child; there is no need to carry any guilt for consenting to the custody being with the other.
- Don't deprive the child of love and affection and the exposure she may get with the other spouse.

- Freedom to the child to interact with the other spouse and his family members protects the child from any kind of stress. It lets the child grow organically.
- Seeing a psychologist/psychiatrist for any behavioural issue is better than losing a relationship.
- Mutually working out a plan for sharing child custody is the best way to work for child's welfare.

A Breakthrough

ANIL WAS ALWAYS impeccably dressed in smart jackets and perfectly matched trousers. His trendy jackets were his USP. He looked a perfect gentleman till he opened his mouth and spewed venom against Ridhi during arguments.

Ridhi, on the other hand, was short, petite, and soft spoken. It always took me an extra effort to comprehend her submissions; she was barely audible. Most times, it was Ridhi's advocate who did the talking on her behalf.

Anil was not represented by any advocate. He was arguing his case personally. He had filed a petition for the custody of Nikki, their six-year-old son, pleading that Nikki's welfare lay with him. He had also prayed for visitation rights at least once a week and overnight custody of Nikki during holidays and festivals such as Diwali, Eid, Muharram, Makar Sankranti, Janmashtami, Mahavir Jayanti, Mahashivratri, Ram Navami, Parsi New Year, Dussehra, Laxmi Pujan, Guru Nanak Jayanti, Raksha Bandhan, Navratri, Ganesh Chaturthi, Anant Chaturdashi, Holi, Independence Day, Republic Day, Children's Day, etc. It seemed as though he had worked really

Anil was always impeccably dressed in smart jackets and perfectly matched trousers.

hard to not miss a single Indian festival or national holiday.

Anil had also prayed that Nikki should spend at least 50 per cent of his summer and winter vacations, as well as Diwali and Christmas vacations, with him. 'I should also be allowed to take Nikki for outings during vacations and on his birthday,' he added.

Nikki had been in the exclusive custody of Ridhi for the last six years, though Anil had been meeting Nikki on and off for short durations. Now, Anil sought to spend 50 per cent of the time with Nikki without sparing a thought for Nikki's willingness or comfort.

Custody time cannot be surgically divided into precise halves. But there was no point in even talking about the same to Anil at that juncture. He was too full of his own grievances against Ridhi and any such conversation with him was meaningless. He strongly felt that he had been unjustly deprived of the custody of his child.

'Ma'am, Ridhi alone has not produced Nikki...I also have the right to spend at least half the time with him. Even my parents and grandmother have the right to interact with him... They love him so much,' submitted Anil, claiming his right as the biological father.

That was not the end of the prayers made by Anil in his petition. He even sought a restraint order against Ridhi to prevent her from taking Nikki to the US, where her parents resided.

'Ma'am, I run a coaching institute for IAS aspirants. I earn a handsome amount. Ridhi cannot provide the kind of education that I can provide to Nikki. I can even personally supervise Nikki's studies, being in the same field,' claimed Anil vide his petition.

During oral submissions, Anil did not leave any stone

unturned in his efforts to convince the court that he deserved Nikki's custody. His loud dispensation hurt my ears. Anil seemed to be under the impression that the louder his volume the better the impact of his submissions, not realising that loud and repetitive arguments become very tedious for the person who is listening.

Anil would always continue in his vociferous style unconcerned about the outcome—whether his arguments made the desired impact or not. He did not pay any attention even to my subtle suggestion that finding fault with every aspect of Ridhi's personality was not at all helping in furthering his plea for custody.

Handling very contentious matrimonial matters has made me realise that ours is a soulful job. It requires absolute attention to deconstruct the drama enacted by spouses and their advocates. It is no less than meditation; one is required to observe and sift through people's emotions to look for the cause of their perceived hurt and trauma. But unlike meditation, it's quite a taxing exercise emotionally and needs robust soul power.

'Ma'am, Ridhi has no time to look after Nikki much less focus on his education,' emphasised Anil.

Then, as if reading my mind that education was not the only criteria to assess the child's welfare, he further added, 'I can even take care of all his other activities.'

'Ridhi's office is in Gurgaon, almost 30 km from her residence. She leaves for office at 8:30 am and returns only by 7:00 pm,' Anil continued haltingly. It seemed as if he was trying to gauge my reaction.

Anil's facial expression left no doubt in my mind that he was seeking my approval for his plea that Ridhi had no time to look after the child.

Anil's submission had made me think about my own routine. I also left home at about 9 o'clock and returned around 6:30 pm. Even after returning, I often needed to spend some time reading files etc. Was I not taking good care of my children? I wondered. A wave of guilt ran through me at a lightning speed, not leaving any part of my being, untouched.

'Ma'am, may I submit...,' a loud address by Anil, brought me back to the matter in hand.

'You know ma'am, Nikki remains with Ridhi's sister, Reema, throughout the day...Her sister has two kids of her own to tend to...She can hardly devote any time or attention to Nikki,' Anil further declared.

'May I say something ma'am,' asked Ridhi, softly seeking permission of the court.

Before I could respond to Ridhi's request, Anil butted in, 'Ma'am, you only tell, won't her sister look after her own two small children first...?'

Ridhi now raised her hand to seek permission to make a submission.

'Ma'am, I have not yet finished...how can she interrupt?' Anil complained, losing his temper.

Anil was quite temperamental, I had observed during the proceedings.

Only after the court's firm direction to let Ridhi complete her submission first, did Anil stop for a while.

'No Ma'am, let him say what he has to say...He has always been like this. It was I, who always bought peace by choosing to stay quiet,' Ridhi mildly reacted, resigning to Anil's emphatic demand that he should be allowed to conclude first.

Despite permission, Ridhi insisted that she would make

her submissions later. She stated this calmly unmoved by the allegations levelled against her by Anil. The words seemed to be coming from a realm of deep stillness within her.

More than deciding the welfare of a child, it is the arguments and counter-arguments of spouses and their advocates, and the drama enacted by them in court, that sap the judge's energy. At such times it is my practice of morning meditation that keeps me in good stead. Connecting with nature during my early morning walks, is the soup for my soul. Nature balances the remnants of the heavy blows of heated arguments with gentle kisses on my cheek. It fills me with gratitude towards life and people who have helped me grow organically. Spouses and advocates appearing before me—some like a jackhammer and some gently—have helped me deal better with my own emotions and taught me profound lessons to ease my life's journey. They have helped me develop my emotional muscles.

A wrought iron bench in the park, where I do my *pranayama*, is like the seat of my power. I feel recharged and in control after my daily routine of breathing exercises and chanting of 'Om'.

'Ma'am, I would ensure not only the best education for Nikki, but also see that he pursued extra-curricular activities like painting, learning some musical instruments...I even have a reputed coach in my vicinity, who is a brown belt holder and teaches Taekwondo to young children...I can pick up and drop Nikki from/to such activities, as my coaching institute is just next to my residence,' Anil added to make yet another point.

Behaving in a little more civilised manner than he normally did, Anil continued, 'Ridhi cannot manage all this...where does she have the time to spend on Nikki and take care of his activities'.

'Nikki is actually being totally neglected by Ridhi,' Anil went back once again to his determined effort to somehow convince me to shift the custody of Nikki to him during the pendency of his custody petition.

'Ma'am, he cannot be allowed to say whatever he wishes to...He cannot take advantage of my silence,' Ridhi finally raised her voice a little, to make her point.

'Ma'am, I have not finished yet,' Anil butted in again.

'Ma'am, he cannot be allowed to have his way always,' interjected Ridhi's lady advocate, a well-mannered young woman, who wore a large powder *bindi*, and was always elegantly dressed. With her receding hairline, it was hard to miss her frown and the creases on her forehead, which were too pronounced.

It did not take me much effort to persuade Ridhi and her advocate to wait for their turn.

Anil was annoyed. He believed that they were interrupting intentionally to break his flow. 'Ma'am, I am not oblivious of the motive behind this... Please give me a moment to recollect what I was saying,' he said asking the court's permission for a few minutes' break. But within no time, he started off again like a rocket.

'Ma'am, the distance from Ridhi's residence to Nikki's school is about 15 kilometres, which is also taking a toll on Nikki's health. Whereas, there are many good schools within a 5 km radius of my house,' Anil made another point.

'...I am still ready to patch up and resolve for Nikki's sake,' said Anil after a brief pause.

This was out of the blue and I was not surprised at Ridhi's reaction.

'Wow...first you torture your wife, make her life miserable, and compel her to leave with a new-born...and then after a few years you want to patch up...Do you even know, what you are saying,' Ridhi reacted sharply.

'Ma'am, I tried adjusting with Anil and his family in every possible manner. But there was no respite from their everyday taunts—whether it was about the standard of the reception given to their guests, the quality of the dowry articles, the amount of *shagun* (cash gift) given to Anil and his close relatives, or the way I dressed up after marriage. Ma'am you cannot even imagine the ways in which I was put down,' Ridhi said sadly trying hard to stem her tears.

Ridhi's grief was so intense that for a moment I was overwhelmed. But somehow I managed to control myself.

Although, unlike other spouses, she was narrating her ill-treatment just as facts, emotions attached to them seemingly got triggered and Ridhi became emotional before she could conclude. After a short pause, Ridhi continued sounding absolutely normal.

'...They did not like my cooking...or even the way I ate... They created a ruckus when I chose a hospital for my delivery. To buy peace, I agreed to register with the hospital chosen by Anil. How long could I have tolerated all this?...Even after Nikki's birth there was so much *hungama*, when I put forth a wish to visit my guruji for his blessings for the new-born. Ultimately, I gave up even on that,' recounted Ridhi.

'Naming the child was another issue which was blown out of proportion. I was thoroughly fed up with my life. I was left with no option, but to leave my matrimonial home. I would have turned insane had I not left,' she added.

'It was under these circumstances that I approached the Crime Against Women (CAW) Cell; that too because I was not allowed to take even our clothes and other essentials. Ma'am, you only tell me, of what use were our clothes and other belongings to him. They were not returned despite directions of the CAW Cell, only to torture me further. Subsequently, Anil handed over some of our clothes and necessary things after four months, when he was pressurised by the CAW Cell. Some of Nikki's clothes were useless by that time, as he had outgrown them,' Ridhi revealed.

'Tell me Ma'am, where was his concern for the child at that time?' asked Ridhi, looking at Anil for an answer.

Ridhi's petition for divorce on grounds of cruelty was also pending.

Anil, who surprisingly was silent till then, suddenly burst out, 'Ma'am, my grandmother and ninety-five-year-old great-grandmother, and other close relatives are being denied access to meet Nikki in order to blackmail me to succumb to Ridhi's unjustified demands for divorce and substantial amount towards the settlement of all the disputes between us.'

Without responding to any of Ridhi's allegations, he continued, 'Ridhi seems to be least bothered about the impact the divorce will have on Nikki's upbringing. Nikki is being kept away from all of us and is even being tutored against us. He is rather being used as a weapon to blackmail us to seek divorce. Such behaviour is deplorable.'

Anil did not stop at that. 'Ma'am, I know who her advisors are...They are brainwashing her in order to fan the animosity between us for their selfish interests without sparing a thought about the damage it is causing to Nikki's growth,' he continued.

How were Ridhi's family members going to benefit from the rift between Anil and Ridhi? What was the advantage they were going to derive? While I was still trying to figure out the same—because Anil didn't bother to tell—Anil continued with his submissions. 'Nikki loves spending time with us, as we have swings in our lawn, which he loves to play on…Ma'am we have even converted a room into an amphitheatre, where Nikki enjoys watching movies and playing video games.'

'To secure Nikki's future, I have even obtained an LIC policy of Rupees twenty lakhs which will help in Nikki's higher education…I have planned for his higher education abroad,' Anil continued further.

Perhaps Anil thought that all the points he had already made had not convinced the court. So he continued further, 'Ma'am, I have no bad habits…I am a teetotaller. To expand Nikki's exposure and his knowledge base and also to strengthen his bond with my family members, I have been taking the family out for vacations. This has immensely contributed to Nikki's personality. Nikki always feels more secure in our company.'

'Ma'am, on many an occasion, during his visits, Nikki has shared that he misses me a lot…even his grandparents and his great grandmother. Not only this, Nikki even mentioned that he did not like to live in his uncle's house where he was neglected. Nikki says that his *maasi* (mother's sister) most of the time remains busy with her own children and that he loves to be in our house, as everyone showers him with love. He is the apple of everyone's eye,' Anil claimed.

'I have even taken membership in a prestigious club, where Nikki can enjoy swimming and many other activities, like watching children's movies. He can participate in various competitions organised by the club. I have also got Ridhi a membership in the club,' he added

'Ma'am all this does not matter now, when there is no love and trust left in our relationship,' interjected Ridhi.

'Ma'am, she is under the influence of her sister and brother-in-law. They have been instigating her against me. But she cannot comprehend what she is doing to Nikki and his life, as she has been totally brainwashed,' retorted Anil.

'Ma'am, she fails to understand that in Indian society, absence of the father will always be questioned,' Anil went on to add, sermonising Ridhi, about the fate she may meet.

Ridhi outwardly paid no attention to Anil's rhetoric.

'Ma'am she does not even appreciate the challenge she might face at the time of getting a marriage alliance for Nikki,' he continued.

'Can you please ask him to stop ma'am...I am fed up of his *gyan* (wisdom),' pleaded Ridhi.

'A person who could not handle his own marriage, who could not respect his relationship with his wife under the influence of his parents, has no right at all to talk about all this. Where was the Indian society when he and his family members tortured me and compelled me to leave with an infant? Where was the society, when he so heartlessly refused to hand over even the child's clothes? Forget my clothes and other essentials. He should be asked to stop immediately. I am fed up now,' said Ridhi angrily.

Anil, who for a change was standing quiet till then with his eyes fixed on the ground, suddenly flew into a rage.

'Ma'am, ask her to stop now! Enough is enough! Otherwise, I will be compelled to disclose everything,' said Anil sounding as if he had some great secret under his sleeve.

'Ma'am, let him 'disclose' whatever he wishes to...let it all be over,' retorted Ridhi.

I intervened before it could get out of hand.

An effort was made to urge Ridhi and Anil to draw a plan, sharing the custody of Nikki.

It is best if spouses themselves draw a shared parenting plan. It helps in avoiding future conflict. It not only saves the child from the trauma of bickering parents, but also saves a lot of the court's time. However, I was not very fortunate as Anil refused to budge from his demands.

Since Anil was contesting his own case, I did not have the advantage of good offices of the advocates of both sides. Ridhi's advocate found it impossible to communicate with Anil. Anil hardly trusted anyone.

Another issue with such litigants, who pursue their own case, is that they are unable to look at any situation objectively, being totally attached to their perceived hurt and view point on everything.

It is actually pretty tough to deal with such litigants, as they don't trust anyone; and always belabour under the impression that they know the best.

Luckily for the child, I got a breakthrough. Anil finally agreed to a parenting plan put across by me, of course subject to some changes. It worked quite well, though there were some hiccups off and on. It surely cut down on a lot of trauma that Nikki would have been subjected to, had there been no consensus between Anil and Ridhi.

Initially, Anil was allowed to meet Nikki for a few hours. Once Nikki became comfortable in the company of Anil, the conditions were relaxed. Gradually Anil was allowed to have overnight custody of Nikki over weekends.

Pending custody petition, the consensual parenting plan worked well to a great extent.

- Everyone is unique and shaped by the environment they have grown up in. Comparisons are surely avoidable.
- Finding fault with everything which a spouse does is a sure recipe for disaster. Successful matrimony calls for respecting the other's ways and choices.
- Looking objectively at things alone can help secure the welfare of the child. Staking claim for equal division of custody time merely because of biological relationship does not help.
- It is not the parents' rights which are to be determined. It's the child's welfare which is to be weighed while deciding custody claims.
- Instead of competing with the spouse, it would be better if the custodial parent is provided the required support by the non-custodial parent.
- While sharing custody, it is advisable to focus on providing love and care to the child, instead of probing him about the other spouse and her/his family or spending time tutoring the child against the other.
- Suspecting the other spouse and his/her family members is surely avoidable.

THE LEGAL PROCESS

Section 6, The Hindu Minority and Guardianship Act, 1956

'Natural guardians of a Hindu minor:– The natural guardian of a Hindu minor, in respect of the minor's person as well as in respect of the minor's property (excluding his or her undivided interest in joint family property), are –

(a) in the case of a boy or an unmarried girl – the father, and after him, the mother: provided that the custody of a minor who has not completed the age of five years shall ordinarily be with the mother;

(b) in the case of an illegitimate boy or an illegitimate unmarried girl – the mother, and after her, the father;

(c) in the case of a married girl – the husband.'

Section 7, The Guardians and Wards Act, 1890

'(1) Where the Court is satisfied that it is for the *welfare of a minor* that an order should be made –

(a) appointing a guardian of his person or property, or both, or

(b) declaring a person to be such a guardian, the Court may make an order accordingly.'

Section 17, The Guardians and Wards Act, 1890

Matters to be considered by the Court in appointing guardian

'(1) In appointing or declaring the guardian of a minor, the Court shall, subject to the provisions of this section, be guided by what, consistently with the law to which the minor is subject, *appears in the circumstances to be for the welfare of the minor.*

(2) In considering what will be for the welfare of the minor, the *Court shall have regard to the age, sex, and religion of the minor, the character and capacity of the proposed guardian* and his nearness of kin to the minor, the *wishes*, if any, of a deceased parent, and any existing or previous relations of the proposed guardian with the minor or his property.

(3) If the minor is old enough to form an intelligent preference, the Court may consider that *preference.*

(4) ...omitted by Act 3 of 1951

(5) The Court shall not appoint or declare any person to be a guardian against his will.'

The Legal Process

PARENTS ARE THE natural guardians of children. But when they live apart, either (the custodial/non-custodial) parent may seek to be appointed guardian and obtain legal custody of the child. The custodial parent with whom the child is living may also seek to be declared the legal guardian of the child. If both the parents are unavailable due to death or otherwise, any relative, grandparent, friend of the parents, or any other person may also seek to be declared as guardian of the child.[15] An unwed mother can also apply for being declared as the legal guardian of her child.[16]

Who can file?

A petition for appointment as guardian and for custody of a child can be filed under Sections 7 and 25 of The Guardians and Wards Act, 1890. Anyone, irrespective of his/her religion,

15 Section 8, The Guardians and Wards Act, 1890

16 ABC Vs The State (NCT of Delhi), (2015) 10 SCC 1

can avail of the remedy provided under these provisions. Vide such petition, one may seek transfer of custody (if the child leaves or is removed from one's custody) or the permanent custody of a child already in that person's custody. A parent or grandparent or anyone else who wants to have custody of the child for a short duration or wants custody at regular intervals such as once a week/fortnight or on weekends or wants to visit the child can file a petition/application under Section 12 of The Guardians and Wards Act, 1890.

An application for temporary custody/visitation rights can also be filed by a non-custodial parent alongside a petition under Sections 7 and 25 of The Guardians and Wards Act by way of an interim relief pending disposal of the petition, as it may take substantial time for decision on the main petition for permanent custody.

Place of filing

Such petition/application has to be filed before the Family Court within whose jurisdiction the child ordinarily resides.[17] The expression 'ordinarily resides' means where the child generally resides. It signifies something more than a temporary residence. A temporary residence at a particular place under compulsion, however long, cannot be termed as place of 'ordinary residence'.

'Ordinarily resides' does not have the same meaning as 'residence at the time of application'. Thus, the residence at the time of application is not decisive of jurisdiction. The legislature used the words 'ordinarily resides' to avoid mischief

---

17 Section 9, The Guardians and Wards Act, 1890

like the minor being secretly removed to some other place and kept at that place under compulsion.

The place of residence of the natural guardian also does not give jurisdiction to the Court under Section 9(1) Guardians And Wards Act.

When a person leaves his residence for good with no intention of returning and goes to some other place to live, the latter becomes his ordinary place of residence.

Notice to other side

On filing of custody/guardianship petition or application for interim custody, notice is required to be issued by the Court, to the other side/other parent/parents/person, in whose custody the child is, seeking his/her response.[18]

In a path-breaking judgment,[19] a Supreme Court bench headed by Justice Vikramajit Sen held that an unwed mother in India can apply to become the sole guardian of a child without giving notice to the father of the child and without disclosing his identity. The Court in that case also directed that if a single parent/unwed mother applies for issuance of a birth certificate for a child born from her womb, the authorities concerned may only require her to furnish an affidavit to this effect, and must thereupon issue the birth certificate, unless there is a court direction to the contrary.

Generally, as soon as the custodial parent/mother receives notice of the custody petition, the first thought which crosses his/her mind is that the child may be snatched from him/

18 Section 11 of The Guardians and Wards Act, 1890

19 ABC Vs The State (NCT of Delhi), (2015) 10 SCC 1

her. It triggers a myriad of emotions leaving him/her very apprehensive. Such a state of mind and anxiety sometimes leads such persons to be exploited by unscrupulous advocates who feed their fears. One need not panic. Courts do not pass any order without hearing the other side. Furthermore, every court order is guided by the welfare and interest of the child.

In case the application for custody is contested or opposed, which is generally the case, the matter is adjourned for reply and arguments. Meanwhile, both the parties are counselled by the Judge and are even referred for counselling to the counsellors attached to the court, depending upon the facts of each case. They may also be referred for mediation to the court's mediation centres.

A meeting with the child is held by the Judge to assess the child's comfort level with the person claiming custody. In case, the child is old enough to make an intelligent choice, her wishes are also to be considered.[20]

If both the spouses on their own or after counselling are able to arrive at an arrangement for sharing custody, a consent order is passed. If they cannot arrive at any consensus, an order is passed by the court after hearing both the sides.

Before passing any order of custody, it is the welfare of the child which has to be assessed. *The welfare of the child is the paramount consideration which guides custody orders.*[21] In case, the court arrives at the conclusion that the person having custody is unable to take care of the child and the welfare of the

20 Section 17(3) The Guardians & Wards Act, Article 12 of the Child Rights Convention 1989 (to which India is signatory)

21 Section 13, The Hindu Minority and Guardianship Act; Section 17 of The Guardians and Wards Act

child lies with the other party, then the custody is directed to be handed over to such a party. In case it is felt that the child is well taken care of by the custodial parent, the custody is generally not disturbed as that may unsettle the child. However, taking into account the facts of each case, the applicant/the non-custodial parent may be allowed to meet the child at regular intervals. Another possibility is that the applicant parent may be allowed to have custody of the child for short durations, like on weekends or holidays at regular intervals, as is convenient to the child.

Welfare of the child

Best interest and welfare of the child is assessed considering what would best serve the child's health (emotional as well as physical), education, and overall development, etc. Interaction with the custodial and non-custodial parent or the person who has custody helps a judge to ascertain what would be in the welfare of the child. Custody and visitation arrangements are worked out after considering the convenience/inconvenience of the custodial/non-custodial parent and the best interest of the child. Such solutions may not always be to the liking of a parent but these have to be in the interest and welfare of the child, which is paramount.

Relevant factors for assessment of welfare of the child

Section 17 of The Guardians and Wards Act prescribes the matters to be considered by the court while assessing the welfare of the child. It says that in considering what will be in the welfare of the minor, the court shall have regard to the age, sex, and religion of the minor, the character and capacity of the proposed guardian and his nearness to the minor, the wishes, if any, of a deceased parent, and any existing or previous relations of the proposed guardian with the minor or his property.

Regarding age, as per law, if the child's age is less than five years, the mother can claim physical custody and the father can have visitation rights. As per Section 6 of The Hindu Minority and Guardianship Act, 1956, custody of a child below the age of five years should ordinarily be with the mother unless she is proven to be unfit for raising the child. The court in one case[22] likened the mother's lap to God's own cradle, as long as the child is young enough to need the mother's day-to-day care. Once the child crosses the age of five, the physical custody and upbringing of the child can be re-considered by the court.

A female child nearing the age of puberty may be allowed to continue to be in the custody of the mother. In one case, the father filed for custody of his eleven-year-old girl child on the ground that the child's mother was having an extramarital affair and the child had seen them in a very intimate position. The petition was strongly contested by the mother on various grounds including the fact that the child had just stepped into puberty and may not be comfortable living with the father. Although the father's allegations seemed to be true, after interviewing the child and keeping in mind her comfort and other facts and circumstances (the fact that she had recently attained puberty), her custody was continued with the mother.

In one case,[23] the father fiercely contested the custody litigation alleging that the mother of the child was involved

---

22 (1993) 2 Hindu LR 506 (Mad)

23 Pawan Kumar Jha Vs Sapna Moudgil, MANU/DE/1136/2004

in extramarital relations; and that the child, when he was two years old, had witnessed his mother in a sexually intimate position with her friend and therefore, she did not deserve to have any interaction with the child.

The High Court, after taking into account the fact that the son was now almost seven years of age and had shown interest in his mother, observed that it would be appropriate to encourage their meeting. The High Court also noted that both parents should make a joint effort to achieve this. However, if one of the parents ie. the father was not inclined to do so, the mother should be permitted to meet the son to develop a better bond. Keeping in mind the best interest of the child, the High Court upheld the order of the lower court allowing the mother and son to meet.

While assessing overall capacity and suitability of a person/ parent for determining the welfare of a child and vesting of its custody in a person, various factors which are taken into account can be summarised as:-

(a) Capacity, financial and otherwise, of the person claiming custody, to take care of the child.
(b) Capacity to provide emotional support and security.
(c) Ability to take care of the child's education and other needs.
(d) Time he/she can spend and his/her availability to the child.
(f) Atmosphere available at the place etc.

Non-payment of maintenance

Non-payment of maintenance by a parent/husband amounts to failure to discharge his moral and legal obligation towards his wife and child, and reflects on the conduct of the father. It may disentitle him from claiming custody and guardianship of the child. The Court, in one case[24] where the father failed to pay the maintenance all along, observed that a person who refuses to pay maintenance to his own child cannot claim to be interested in betterment of the child. The Court frowned upon the response of the father that he would look after the future and career of the child. The Court noted that bona fides are not to be seen from what is said, but are to be seen from what is done.

If the intention of the parent not paying maintenance is suspect, he cannot be stated to be suitable for the custody of the child.

Murder-accused mother given custody

The character of the person claiming custody is one of the criteria to assess the welfare of the child. To fully appreciate that, many attendant facts are to be kept in mind.

'M' was accused of killing her husband and was out on bail. On her petition, the Delhi High Court directed the grandparents to hand over the custody of the minor daughter to the mother 'M', noting that the best interest of the school-going child lay with the mother.

'M' had pleaded that she was already taking care of the younger child and had the support of her parents and brother. She was an established businesswoman who earned well prior to the death of her husband and also owned two flats.

---

24 Ayub Khan Vs. Saira Begum I (2002) DMC 237

The court noted that a mother cannot be deprived of custody merely on the allegation of murdering her husband; and also because her in-laws could not point out any other reason why she should be divested of custody. The court however directed the mother to ensure that the child's schooling was not disrupted.

Before handing over the custody, the Court allowed the mother to meet the minor child in the presence of a mediator at the Mediation and Conciliation Centre of the High Court, as they had been separated for more than six months.[25]

The High Court hoped that a prior meeting before getting custody would help them form a bond, even as it ordered the police to ensure that law and order was maintained and no ruckus was created by the in-laws.

Father accused of dowry death denied custody

In another case,[26] the father of a minor son aged about six years was allegedly responsible for the death of the child's mother on account of her torture for dowry and was charged under Sections 498-A and 304-B of Indian Penal Code. He was declined custody of the child by the Supreme Court.

After being enlarged on bail, the father filed an application for custody of the boy who was with his maternal grandparents at that time. The trial court as well as the High Court allowed the application and directed the maternal grandparents to immediately hand over custody of the minor to the father. The

25 Nazmeen Khan Vs Govt. of NCT of Delhi, WP (Crl) 2431/18, Judgement dated 27 August 2018

26 Nil Ratan Kundu and Another Vs Abhijit Kundu, (2008) 9 SCC 413

Supreme Court, after considering the factual matrix of the case, set aside the order of the courts below, observing that:

> '52. ...the law relating to custody of a child is fairly well settled and it is this: in deciding a difficult and complex question as to the custody of a minor, a court of law should keep in mind the relevant statutes and the rights flowing therefrom. But such cases cannot be decided solely by interpreting legal provisions. In dealing with custody cases, is neither bound by statutes nor by strict rules of evidence or procedure nor by precedents. In selecting proper guardian of a minor, the paramount consideration should be the welfare and well-being of the child. In selecting a guardian, the court is exercising parens patriae jurisdiction and is expected, nay bound, to give due weight to a child's ordinary comfort, contentment, health, education, intellectual development, and favourable surroundings. But over and above physical comforts, moral and ethical values cannot be ignored.
>
> They are equally, or we may say, even more important, essential, and indispensable considerations. If the minor is old enough to form an intelligent preference or judgment, the court must consider such preference as well, though the final decision should rest with the court as to what is conducive to the welfare of the minor.
>
> 58. ...Though this Court in Rosy Jacob held that children are not mere chattels nor toys, the trial court directed handing over custody of Antariksh 'immediately' by removing him from the custody of his maternal grandparents. Similarly, the High Court, which had stayed the order of the trial court during the pendency of appeal, ordered handing over Antariksh to his father within twenty-four hours positively. We may only

state that a child is not 'property' or 'commodity'. To repeat, issues relating to custody of minors and tender-aged children have to be handled with love, affection, sentiments, and by applying human touch to the problem.

62. Now, it has come in evidence that after the death of Mithu (mother of Antariksh) and lodging of first information report by her father against Abhijit (father of Antariksh) and his mother (paternal grandmother of Antariksh), Abhijit was arrested by the police. It was also stated by Nil Ratan Kundu (father of Mithu) that mother of accused Abhijit (paternal grandmother of Antariksh) absconded and Antariksh was found sick from the house of Abhijit.

64. Thus, a complaint against the father alleging and attributing the death of the mother, and a case under Section 498-A IPC is indeed a relevant factor and a court of law must address the said circumstance while deciding the custody of the minor in favour of such a person. To us, it is no answer to state that in case the father is convicted, it is open to the maternal grandparents to make an appropriate application for change of custody. Even at this stage, the said fact ought to have been considered and an appropriate order ought to have been passed.

72. We have called Antariksh in our chamber. To us, he appeared to be quite intelligent. When we asked him whether he wanted to go to his father and to stay with him, he unequivocally refused to go with him or to stay with him. He also stated that he was very happy with his maternal grandparents and would like to continue to stay with them. We are, therefore, of the considered view that it would not be proper on the facts and in the circumstances to give custody of Antariksh to his father,

the respondent herein.'

The Supreme Court, taking note of the above factors viz. nature of allegations against the father, conduct of the father, the absconding of the grandmother leaving the sick child behind, and the choice of the child declined custody to the father.

Incarcerated mother may have custody of child in jail

There may be cases where a woman prisoner delivers the child while in custody or is incarcerated while the child is an infant and cannot be weaned away from the feeding mother. In such situations, a child may be given in custody of the mother inside the prison. Ideally no child shall be admitted into or retained in prison if he/she has attained the age of six years, unless no other arrangement for keeping the child with relatives or otherwise is available. The Delhi Prison Rules, 2018, spell out the arrangements for the custody of children of prisoners in such situations. These rules provide that once they attain the age of six years, the children have to be sent to a child care institution, where they have to be kept until the mother is released or the child becomes an adult. These children are allowed to meet their mothers twice a week.

The rules also emphasise that where the child has been inside a prison with the mother and has crossed the age of six and needs to be removed from the present environment, they must be removed from the mother's care with utmost sensitivity. The prison administration should ensure that links between inmates and children outside prison are maintained throughout the incarceration.

The place of interaction between inmates and their children living outside prison should be one where easy conversation can take place, in a positive environment, where physical contact is possible between mother and child.

The rules also require the prison administration to ensure holistic development of children of inmates confined in the prisons. To the extent possible, the prison administration shall strive to create a suitable environment for the children's upbringing which is as close as possible to that of a child outside prison. The Board of Visitors shall inspect these facilities at regular intervals.

Sexual abuse allegations

At times, the custodial spouse/wife alleges inappropriate behaviour of the other spouse/father and emphatically resists meetings with the father, leave alone interim custody. In one such case, the wife filed a psychiatrist's report pleading that the child was taken for counselling because of the father's unexplained odd behaviour. Such allegations have to be dealt with great circumspection as the possibility of such charges being trumped up by a vindictive parent to deprive the other of custody/visitation rights or to take revenge, cannot be ruled out.

No doubt, such serious allegations cannot be brushed aside lightly. But at the same time, it has to be kept in mind, that the more serious the allegations, the higher the standard of proof called for. Such allegations need to be dealt with very carefully.[27]

In such situations after making an independent assessment, the accused father can be allowed to meet the child, if the court feels, under the supervision of a counsellor and in the children's room attached to the Family Court.

---

27 Sudesh Jhaku Vs KCJ 62 (1996) DLT 5639

Any of the parties aggrieved by an order deciding guardianship, custody, or visitation rights, can challenge the same before the concerned High Court.

SUGGESTIONS

Pre-litigation counselling

The contest for custody and declaration as guardian directly impacts the child's psyche. This process can be made a little less traumatic for all the stakeholders, most importantly the child, who is the central point of this litigation, if an intervention is made before initiation of such litigation.

Thus, anyone intending to file a custody petition should first be referred for counselling. The law should be explained to them. They should be apprised that the needs and welfare of the child come first and over and above their own concerns. The counsellor should explain to them that custody does not mean exclusive ownership of the child. Sharing custody actually means sharing responsibility for the best upbringing of the child.

The counsellor can endeavour to explain to the custodial parent that participation of both the parents in all areas of the child's life, be it upbringing, health, education, medical attention, other interests, special talents, etc. goes a long way in the all-round development of a child's personality. The counsellor can play an instrumental role in explaining to the custodial parent that any grievance against the non-custodial parent should not come in the way of welfare of the child.

Most of the times, rather almost all the time, the resistance to sharing of child's custody is because of one's own hurt at the hands of the other. Even the children resist meeting the other parent because that parent is painted black by the custodial parent. The child is vulnerable to tutoring by either or both the parents.

Therefore, pre-litigation counselling can go a long way. Audio-video tools can be used during such counselling to demonstrate the impact of a tug of war between parents on children. It can also explain visually, the anxiety which the child may undergo by the very intimidating environment of the court despite housing the Family Courts in separate buildings away from regular courts and creation of special children's rooms. Children are often scared when they are subjected to interaction/interview by the counsellor and the judge/ or judges, in case of change of judge. Audio-video clips can demonstrate how anxiety in the children sets in the moment they are prepared for a court visit.

Workshops for Advocates

Advocates keep updating themselves on the latest developments in the field of law. It would go a long way, if some workshops are organised for their sensitisation to children's vulnerabilities in such situations; how they can guide their clients about the impact of such litigation on children. Such workshops may also include talks on child psychology. If such workshops are attended by both the clients and the advocates together, these may make the task of the advocates a bit easier in communicating with their clients/parents, on such issues.

As far as Family Court Judges are concerned, such workshops and training programmes are regularly held. Maybe, a little more focus can be had on human/child psychology given the special/sensitive nature of these courts. Ideally, while posting judges to Family Courts, their inclination, suitability, and sensitivity towards such issues, should be kept in mind.

Once a custody petition is filed despite counselling, efforts are made even by courts to work out an amicable solution.

Sharing custody – Co-parenting

To avoid filing of repeated applications for sharing of custody during holidays or on social and religious occasions, it is advisable to draw up a co-parenting plan with the assistance of both the parents, right at the beginning, ie. when the other party appears after notice.

It is a herculean task to persuade parents to agree to fair co-parenting plans. Both detest the idea of cooperating with a person who is seen as a tormentor and responsible for the situation. The question often asked is, how could a person responsible for their separation be allowed to meet the child, much less share the custody, that too for equal time?

Experience shows that even if such a plan is prepared with the consent of both the parents, it is no guarantee of peaceful sharing of custody. But it does help in saving the child from repeated appearances and saves the court's precious judicial time. A slight deviation from timings fixed for such meetings is perceived as deliberate impingement of one's allotted time. On other occasions, there is a tussle about the quality of time spent due to the presence of the parent or a counsellor or the ambience of the meeting place.

In one case, considering the child's comfort as he was meeting his father after a long hiatus, the presence of a grandparent, at a distance, was permitted. The father had earlier complained that he was not able to spend quality time with his child because the child remained distracted by the presence of the mother. The father failed to appreciate that the child was very hesitant in meeting him after a long gap and needed the comforting presence of the custodial parent. Since the father strongly objected to this, the presence of a maternal grandparent was allowed in that situation.

Ideally, both the parents must get to participate in bringing up the child; both should be able to share the joy of being part of the child's life. Many guidelines in this respect have been issued by higher courts from time to time through their judgments. Even NGOs working in the area of child rights[28] have done extensive work in this field.

Recently, in July 2019, Save Child India Foundation filed a petition[29] before the Honourable Supreme Court raising the issue – Can 'joint parenting' be adopted in India so that a child could be looked after by both parents after divorce instead of one receiving custody and primary responsibility to do so?

Though, a bench of Justices SA Bobde and BR Gavai was initially reluctant in entertaining the PIL (Public Interest Litigation) on joint parenting, saying Parliament can frame a law rather than the judiciary, it relented and issued notice to the Centre seeking response on the petition seeking framing of guidelines or an amendment of law.

---

28 Child Rights Foundations, Mumbai, India, prepared Child Access and Custody Guidelines covering various aspects of custody and visitation rights of both partners.

29 PIL No. 873/2019 – Save Child India Foundation Vs. Union of India

The Supreme Court agreed to examine such a possibility in order to protect the interests of children who have to go through mental trauma when parents are entangled in a custody battle.

How to divide time – half & half?

Co-parenting is not and cannot be a mathematical fifty-fifty.

Many a times, the non-custodial parent, mostly the father, insists upon absolute half and half time-share arrangement. It is insisted that the child should live with him for minimum three days a week or the child should come to him on Friday afternoon and leave for school on Monday from his house.

After spending a week at school, the child looks forward to some *masti* (fun) time. But it is time to pack up and leave for the other parent's house. Any delay can expose the custodial parent to the risk of facing contempt. The child does not remain untouched by the custodial parent's anxiety and is compelled to pack up her bags and is not allowed to take her own time.

When the child reaches the other parent, she needs some time to relax. At the back of her mind, the child carries the thought that she has to ensure that the parent, who has got company on weekends, is happy. The child feels obliged to strike up a conversation with everyone in that family, which takes quite an effort. This kills the spontaneity of the child. By the time the child adapts to the setup and gets into weekend mode, it is time to pack up and go back to the other parent.

Where should the child unwind after a gruelling week at school? Where should they keep their personal stuff to enjoy during the weekend? Instead of a happy time, the whole exercise may turn out to be an annoying drill. This can be deeply unsettling for the child.

The child may end up with a feeling of just getting in and out from one role to another with no 'leisure' time. Such an arrangement may leave the child more distraught than being with one parent alone. It amounts to tugging the child in opposite directions. Can we expect children to be happy with such arrangements? What is the way out?

The Supreme Court has disapproved of such orders which reduce the child to a 'shuttlecock'.[30] It observed that a child cannot be tossed like a shuttlecock.

Without total understanding (which is very difficult to expect) and cooperation of both parents, even the best 'parenting plan' will fail to achieve the goal of 'shared parenting'. I am reminded of the contest before King Solomon between two women, both of who claimed to be the mother of the same child. Solomon ruled that the child be split in two, each woman receiving half of the child. One of them cried out that the baby should not be killed but be given to the other. Whereas, the other woman sought the child's division. Solomon found the true mother to be the one who pleaded not to kill. The situation before the courts is often similar, as both the parents pull the child towards themselves, claiming an exact half.

Partnership of both parents in a child's upbringing as contemplated by law is not mathematical. That is why the law provides the principle of welfare of the child and not the equal right of parents. No doubt, parents can't be deprived of the joy of participating in bringing up their child. But it is quite a task

30 KSM Karthikeya Vs G Renukadevi (SLP No. 4855/2014) Judgement dated 18 July 2014; Dipper Vs Dipper (1980) 2All E.R.722.

to make them understand that it is about caring for the child rather than possessing him. Recently a national daily[31] reported that Shah Rukh Khan said that he believed in sharing parental responsibilities. On being asked about the bringing up of her six-year-old son AbRam, as she herself is a working mother, Gauri Khan reportedly said, 'Shah Rukh and I share his time. He is with Shah Rukh for three days, and for the remaining four, he is with me. That gives me enough time to do my work. We believe in sharing parenting responsibilities. So, I would say, it has been a cakewalk.'

Such camaraderie often goes missing in the event of estrangement between spouses.

Recently, reportedly[32], a PIL has been filed in the Supreme Court by London-based NRI activist Ms Sulochana Rani seeking directions of the Supreme Court to develop the concept of 'shared parenting' keeping in mind the welfare of the kids. Petitioner has pleaded that the legal provisions which currently exist as per various personal laws are in the nature of entrusting the custody of children exclusively to one of the parents in case of separation, overlooking their welfare and fundamental right to have 'care and love of both the parents'. The petitioner referred to the Muslim Personal Law (Shariat) Application Act, 1937, according to which the father is considered as the guardian of the child and the mother gets automatic custody only for five years after the birth of the kids. The Supreme Court agreed to examine the constitutional validity of certain provisions of various Hindu and Muslim personal laws and issued the notice to the Central government.

31 Delhi Times, (A Times of India Publication), 21 May 2019
32 The Times of India, Delhi dated 26 October 2019

Child's preference

Law requires that if children are old enough to form an intelligent preference about who they wish to stay with, for how long, and whether they wish to meet the non-custodial parent, the court may consider the child's preference.

To elicit the child's view remains a challenge. For this purpose, meetings are held with children as well as both parents. Great care is called for during interactions with the child. It may be very traumatic for the child to either choose between parents or to choose time slots to be spent with both, leaving no scope for living organically. Children feel pressured and anxious lest they annoy any of the parents; they want the best from both. The child may feel scared of being judged as 'pro' or 'anti' any parent, on expressing any choice. This whole exercise of having to meet the lawyer, the judge, the counsellor, and being interviewed by them, renders children very anxious and nervous leading to psychosomatic ailments like giddiness, lack of appetite, loss of interest in studies and even in playful activities. Further, the pressure of making a choice and fear of being misunderstood and judged may leave children totally exhausted.

In one case, a boy named Babu during counselling sessions readily agreed to spend weekends with his father, who lived with his parents. He thoroughly enjoyed his father's company. However, when Babu went to stay with the father, his grandparents would paint his mother black. On returning to his mother's place, Babu was subjected to sustained interrogation about the time spent at the father's place. The poor child unknowingly shared his grandparents' views about the mother. Lo! All hell broke loose on the next date of hearing. The mother strongly objected to sending him to his father's home on the ground that the grandparents were poisoning Babu's mind against her. This not only made the father's situation awkward but also made the judge's task very difficult. Due to so much of hostility around, Babu also was scared of visiting his father again. On the next date, the mother did not bring Babu, pleading that he was sick. On the date thereafter, Babu seemed reluctant to accompany his father and said that he wanted to return home after meeting his father in court or elsewhere for a few hours. Another meeting with Babu was held, but nothing better could be worked out.

Then the judge was transferred. Babu found it very unsettling to share his story all over again with the next judge.

Calling children for repeated meetings may be traumatic for them. After meeting two-three judges, Babu became rebellious and finally refused to go to court. His behaviour in school also changed, which made the mother's job difficult.

It's a humongous task to elicit the genuine choice of the child. It's a very delicate exercise to scan whether the child's hostility to any parent is his own or is the result of tutoring. Tutoring is not always an overt act. It can be very subtle and accomplished over a period of time. Hostility, even when not injected, is generally seen to be because of perceived behaviour of the non-custodial parent towards the custodial parent. Children may not truly understand the nuances or dynamics of spousal behaviour towards each other. They may be governed by their own immature conclusions due to lack of ability to analyse such behaviour.

Then there is also the question whether the child knows its own welfare. His choice may be totally coloured by a picture of the other parent painted to him over a long period of time.

The welfare of the child being central, which includes knowing both parents, receiving their love and affection and also that of extended families on both sides, has to be kept in mind while considering the child's choice. Therefore, considering the child's choice does not mean mindless agreement with it. The child may be of age but may not be equipped to deal with the situation and may have difficulty choosing between beloved parents.

In some instances of international abduction, the children may want to stay in the country to which they are brought as they enjoy being with the extended family. But, children's wishes may be ignored in view of violation by the custodial parent of a shared parenting plan, agreed before the court.

Age of intelligence

There is no fixed age at which a child is allowed to choose. The age at which a child can be said to be able to form an intelligent preference varies and much depends on the judge's interaction with the child. In one case, the older brother was thirteen and the younger only eight. But I found the younger to be more articulate than his elder sibling. He was very clear about his preference and choice. Whereas, the elder one seemed very restrained and unclear.

One has to be very cautious. Financial considerations may influence the children to choose one parent over the other. In one case, a child left the mother because she refused to buy him an iPad whereas the father pampered him with whatever gadget he demanded. The mother was very distraught and depressed that her son had chosen his father over her. Even a parent's disciplinarian approach and denial of such indulgences for the child's own good may influence the child's choice. Children therefore, may not know what is best for them. Such cases stress out a judge in passing custody orders as per law, which may go against the child's emphatic choice.

I am also reminded of a peculiar case where the child happily met the father in the first meeting after a court order. However, during subsequent meetings, the child seemed distanced and it took the father quite an effort to spend meaningful time with his son. Later, at his request, the father was given weekend custody. Surprisingly, after spending a weekend with his father, the son refused to go back to the mother. This created serious apprehensions in the mother's mind and triggered allegations from her side that the child had been tutored by the father. The father somehow persuaded the child to go back to the mother. Once the child returned to the mother, to the shock and dismay of the father, the child, resisted visiting him on the weekends.

A conversation with the child revealed that the child loved both the parents. He felt settled with the parent he lived with for a few days and felt unsettled on being moved out to the other. That was the reason he preferred to continuously stay with one parent instead of shuttling between the two. This is a glimpse of the fate children meet, even when they have loving interactions with the parents.

Children at times are left exhausted trying to please both the parents. Basically, the children yearn to be with both. They feel imprisoned in regimented meetings that leave no scope for mood changes or for life to flow organically [*Ki jidhar ki mauj aye udhar chal do* (go wherever the wave takes you)]. Even genuine resistance of the child to meet the other, as per court order, generally triggers initiation of contempt proceedings.

Contempt actions

Parents invoke contempt jurisdiction when the custody orders are not complied with, alleging deliberate attempt of the custodial parent to keep the child away and not sending him/her for the scheduled meeting or not observing scheduled timings. Such petitions are fiercely defended by the custodial parent pleading child's sickness, unexpected school trip, excess homework, and many other such reasons for the inability of the child to meet during scheduled hours. Allegations against the non-custodial parent are generally about not sending the child back after scheduled hours of meeting.

It is also true that many a times the child herself does not wish to meet the other parent as she finds it difficult to deal with the emotional outburst of that parent. Children feel burdened to deal with complex and emotional issues of the parents and their own feelings. In such situations, there is no scope for issuance of contempt. Even otherwise, it may be too harsh a remedy. In the long run, this may only complicate the issues. Moreover, any order of custody is never final and can always be modified in the light of changed circumstances.

In one case, a mother, in order to protect her custody of the child, was trying to be extra good with him; too much of it was making the child drift away from her; he was finding this behaviour unnatural. The mother was at a loss to understand why the child wanted to spend more time with the father and even refused to return on certain occasions. She emphatically argued that it was all the father's doing. Her point was there is no way the child could have drifted away from her, when she was showering the child with so much love and affection.

In another case, the child preferred to spend more time

with the father who never scolded him, not even when he spent hours in front of a screen. A child may choose a parent who is chilled out in his parenting methods over one who is very strict.

All such aspects have to be kept in mind not only while evaluating the child's choice but also while deciding contempt petitions/custody petitions. Though the child's choice matters before any decision to shift the custody is taken, the whole gamut of facts and complex emotions have to be factored in.

To summarise, a very skilful analysis of the facts and behaviour is called for by a Family Court Judge, in the process of ascertaining what would be in the welfare of the child. Active assistance of advocates is also invaluable. But due to adverse interests of the parties, even well-meaning advocates find themselves unable to facilitate an amicable solution, lest they are misunderstood as siding with the other side. Such situations expose the vulnerability of children, because parents are not willing to listen to either their advocates, or to the court, or the counsellor.

Parents generally, instead of focussing on working out a solution, get busy with their own battles. In one parent's zeal to obtain custody and the other's obsession to somehow resist the same, it becomes nearly impossible to balance all interests. Warring parents want equal time with the children, right down to the last hour and minute. The non-custodial parent wants more quality time with the child and the custodial parent wants a greater financial/other contribution from such a parent. Such parents fail to appreciate that children cannot be treated as divisible assets. This can be deeply discomforting and unsettling for the child.

Avoidable actions

Experience has shown that on being deprived of visitation/ custody, the parents get desperate and try to meet children in any which way.

Meeting children at school

There are cases where the deprived parent tries to meet the children at school. In one such case, the mother got to know that the father had visited the children at school. She created a hue and cry in the court and sought a restraint order. She even wrote to the school, giving details of their case pending before the court, warning them that the school shall be responsible if anything happens to the child. Such behaviour not only poses trouble for the other parent but also causes immense embarrassment to the children. Personally, I am against parents visiting children at school as I feel such clandestine meetings subject the children to stress and embarrassment.

Non acceptance of gifts

Another drama which is enacted in courts is when the non-custodial parent brings a gift for the child on her birthday or on any other festival. The child refuses to receive it and looks at the custodial parent for approval. In such cases, the common refrain of the custodial parent is that the other has never bothered to look after the child and now simply to impress the child has brought the gift. There have been cases where custodial parents not only throw away such gifts but also create a ruckus in the court.

In one case, the wife alleged that the husband had beaten their son as he had accepted a fountain pen from her on his birthday. The Judge spoke to the child, found that the allegations were true, and directed transfer of custody of the son to the mother. However, in the appeal, the order was modified considering the totality of facts and circumstances.[33]

International Abductions

The Hague Convention of 25 October 1980 on the Civil Aspects of International Child Abduction (Hague Abduction Convention) is a multilateral treaty which deals with the removal/abduction of children from one country to another. It obligates the member countries to protect children internationally from the harmful effects of their wrongful removal or retention; and to establish procedures to ensure their prompt return to the State of their habitual residence as well as to secure protection for rights of access. India is not a signatory to the Hague Abduction Convention.

There are cases where matrimonial disputes arise between Indian citizens living abroad or an Indian citizen settled abroad with a foreign spouse. In such situations, one of the spouses may return to India along with the child, with or without the consent of the other spouse. In such an eventuality, the other parent approaches the court of the foreign country, obtains an order for return of the child, and seeks governmental intervention to obtain custody. Armed with such an order of a foreign court, the parent may also approach an Indian court for return of the child, quoting the order of the foreign court.

The Courts in India in such situations are generally governed by the best interest of the child, considering the attending facts

33 Rosy Jacob Vs Jacob A Chakramakhal AIR 1973 SC 2090

and circumstances of each case. In one such case,[34] the parties after their marriage in India settled in the United Kingdom. They were blessed with a daughter who was born in India. After the birth, the parties went back to the United Kingdom. There were differences between the spouses but they pulled on, the mother of the child going back and forth between India and the UK. When the daughter was about six years of age, the mother came back to India along with the daughter because of the alleged violent behaviour of the father of the child. After about five months of her stay in India, the mother filed a complaint with a Crime Against Women Cell, which issued notice to the father of the child. Thereafter, the father filed a custody petition, allegedly as a counter blast, before the High Court of Justice, Family Division, United Kingdom, seeking return of the daughter. The UK court passed an ex parte order directing the mother to return to the UK along with the child. The father thereafter also filed a writ of habeas corpus before the Delhi High Court.

The High Court directed the mother to comply with the order of the High Court of Justice, Family Division, UK within three weeks and handover the custody of the daughter to the father. The High Court passed the said order holding that the foreign court had the most intimate contact with the child and would be better placed to appreciate the social and cultural milieu in which the child had been brought up. It noted that since the mother had not sought the custody of the child by approaching any competent Indian court prior to the passing of the order by the UK court, therefore, the first effective order/

34 Nithya Anand Raghavan Vs State of NCT of Delhi (2017) 8 SCC 454

directions had been passed by the UK/Foreign court. So, it held that, by applying the principle of comity of courts, the balance of favour would lie with the UK court. It also observed that it would be in the best interest of the child to return to the UK, as she had spent most of her life there and even studied there.

The order of the High Court was challenged by the mother before the Supreme Court. The Supreme Court after detailed discussion of law on the point, declined any directions to the mother to return the seven-year-old girl child to the father taking into account that the girl, who was diagnosed with some heart condition, was staying in India along with her mother, her grandparents, other family members, and relatives unlike in the UK, where she lived in a nuclear family with no extended family. The court also noted that the girl child had been going to school in India for the past one year and had spent equal time in both the countries, out of the first six years. The Court concluded that the child would be more comfortable and secure with her mother, who could provide her love, understanding, care, and guidance for the complete development of her character, personality, and talents.

The Supreme Court also observed that being a girl child, the guardianship of the mother was of utmost significance; ordinarily, the custody of a 'girl' child who is around seven years of age, must ideally be with her mother unless there are circumstances to indicate that it would be harmful for her to remain in custody of her mother. The Court also noted that no such material or evidence had come on record in the case except the fact that the mother had violated the order of the UK court directing her to return the child to the UK. The Court further observed that no restraint order existed when the mother returned to India and the order by the UK court was passed only subsequently.

The Supreme Court while referring to the decision of its three-judge bench in Dr V Ravi Chandran's case[35] observed that:

> '25. ... in Dr V Ravi Chandran (supra)...three-judge bench observed thus:
>
> '27. ...it was also held that **whenever a question arises** before a court **pertaining to the custody of a minor child, the matter is to be decided not on considerations of the legal rights of the parties but on the sole and predominant criterion of what** would best serve the interest of the minor.' (emphasis supplied)...
>
> 26. The consistent view of this court is that **if the child has been brought within India,** the courts in India may conduct a) summary inquiry or b) an elaborate inquiry on the question of custody. Court **may deem it fit to order return of the child** to the country from where he/she was removed **unless such return is shown to be harmful to the child.** In other words, even in the matter of a summary inquiry, **it is open to the court to decline the relief of return** of the child to the country from where he/she was removed **irrespective of a pre-existing order of return of the child by a foreign court.** In an elaborate inquiry, **the court is obliged to examine the merits as to where the paramount interests and welfare of the child lay and reckon the fact of a pre-existing order of the foreign court for return of the child as only one of the circumstances.** In either case, the crucial question to be considered by the court (in the country to which the child is removed) is to answer the issue according to the child's welfare. That has to be done bearing in mind the totality of facts and circumstances of each case independently. Even on close scrutiny of the

35 Nithya Anand Raghavan's case (2017) 8 SCC 454

several decisions pressed before us, we do not find any contra view in this behalf. **The principle of comity of courts cannot be given primacy or more weightage for deciding the matter of custody or for return of the child to the native state.**

29. Once again, we may hasten to add that the decision of the court, in each case, must depend on the totality of the facts and circumstances of the case brought before it whilst considering the welfare of the child which is of paramount consideration. **The order of the foreign court must yield to the welfare of the child.** Further, the remedy of writ of habeas corpus cannot be used for mere enforcement of the directions given by the foreign court against a person within its jurisdiction and convert that jurisdiction into that of an executing court.

30. In a habeas corpus petition as aforesaid, the High Court must examine at the threshold whether the minor is in lawful or unlawful custody of another person (private respondent named in the writ petition). For considering that issue, in a case such as the present one, it is enough to note that the private **respondent was none other than the natural guardian of the minor being her biological mother. Once that fact is ascertained, it can be presumed that the custody of the minor with his/her mother is lawful.** In such a case, only in exceptionable situation, the custody of the minor (girl child) may be ordered to be taken away from her mother for being given to any other person including the husband (father of the child), in exercise of writ jurisdiction. Instead, **the other parent can be asked to resort to a substantive prescribed remedy for getting custody of the child.**

31. The next question to be considered by the High Court would be whether an order passed by the foreign court, directing the mother to produce the child before

it, would render the custody of the minor unlawful? Indubitably, merely because such an order is passed by the foreign court, the custody of the minor would not become unlawful per se.

31. ...it is noticed that **it is an ex parte order passed against the mother after recording prima facie satisfaction that the minor was wrongfully removed from England.** Even on a fair reading of this order, it is not possible to hold that the custody of the minor with her mother has been declared to be unlawful. At best, the appellant may have violated the direction to return the minor to England...'

Thus, it is the best interest of the child which lies at the heart of the custody order.

Conclusion

Custody litigation is a lot about perceptions. There are crafty women who misuse the law and tutor children, just as there are fathers who fight for custody only to avoid any claim by the child for a share in their property or for maintenance or to intimidate the mother into giving up claims of maintenance and alimony, in order to protect her child from the stress of litigation.

'Welfare is not just about money and physical comfort, but also about the moral and religious welfare of the child,' held the Madras High Court.[36] Mrs Annie Besant, President of the Theosophical Society, watched J Krishnamurthi and his brother playing at the beach. She sensed a great potential in them. She approached the boys' father to take charge of them and provide them education in England. The father consented.

36 Mrs Annie Besant vs G Narayaniah [(1913) 25 MLJ 661].

However, later, alleging that the boys had been subjected to inappropriate behaviour, their father changed his mind and sought their return. The Madras High Court directed return of the two brothers, Krishnamurthi and Nityananda. This was challenged before the Privy Council.

The Privy Council set aside the judgment of the Madras High Court on the ground of jurisdiction. The children were interviewed by court order; they stated that they did not want to return to India without completing their education at Oxford.

Where a child rejects a parent and the child's choice is respected by the court, the parent often has a strong reaction to this unexpected powerlessness. But there is no other way except counselling.

WHAT THE LAW SAYS

Laws

The Guardianship and Wards Act, 1890

Section 7:

Power of the Court to make order as to guardianship:–

(1) Where the Court is satisfied that it is for the welfare of a minor that an order should be made –

(a) appointing a guardian of his person or property or both, or

(b) declaring a person to be such a guardian the Court may make an order accordingly.

(2) An order under this section shall imply the removal of any guardian who has not been appointed by will or other instrument or appointed or declared by the Court.

(3) Where a guardian has been appointed by will or other instrument or appointed or declared by the Court, an order under this section appointing or declaring another person to be guardian in his stead shall not be

made until the powers of the guardian appointed or declared as aforesaid have ceased under the provisions of this Act.

Section 8:

Persons entitled to apply for order:– An order shall not be made under the last foregoing section except on the application of –

(a) the person desirous of being, or claiming to be, the guardian of the minor; or
(b) any relative or friend of the minor; or
(c) the Collector of the district or other local area within which the minor ordinarily resides or in which he has property; or
(d) the Collector having authority with respect to the class to which the minor belongs.

Section 9:

Court having jurisdiction to entertain application:–

(1) If the application is with respect to the guardianship of the person of the minor, it shall be made to the District Court having jurisdiction in the place where the minor ordinarily resides.
(2) If the application is with respect to the guardianship of the property of the minor, it may be made either to the District Court having jurisdiction in the place where the minor ordinarily resides or to a District Court having jurisdiction in a place where he has property.
(3) If an application with respect to the guardianship of the property of a minor is made to a District Court

other than that having jurisdiction in the place where the minor ordinarily resides, the Court may return the application if in its opinion the application would be disposed of more justly or conveniently by any other District Court having jurisdiction.

Section 12:

Power to make interlocutory order for production of minor and interim protection of person and property:–

(1) The court may direct that the person, if any, having the custody of the minor, shall produce him or cause him to be produced at such place and time and before such person as it appoints, and may make such order for the temporary custody and protection of the person or property of the minor as it thinks proper.

(2) If the minor is a female who ought not to be compelled to appear in public, the direction under sub-section (1) for her production shall require her to be produced in accordance with the customs and manners of the country.

(3) Nothing in this section shall authorise—

   (a) the court to place a female minor in the temporary custody of a person claiming to be her guardian on the ground of his being her husband, unless she is already in his custody with the consent of her parents, if any, or

   (b) any person to whom the temporary custody and protection of the property of a minor is entrusted to dispossess otherwise than by due course of law any person in possession of any of the property.

Section 17:

Matters to be considered by the Court in appointing guardian:–

(1) In appointing or declaring the guardian of a minor, the Court shall, subject to the provisions of this section, be guided by what, consistently with the law to which the minor is subject, appears in the circumstances to be for the welfare of the minor.

(2) In considering what will be for the welfare of the minor, the Courts shall have regard to the age, sex, and religion of the minor, the character and capacity of the proposed guardian and his nearness of kin to the minor, the wishes, if any, of a deceased parent, and any existing or previous relations of the proposed guardian with the minor or his property.

(3) If the minor is old enough to form an intelligent preference, the Court may consider that preference.

(4) The Court shall not appoint or declare any person to be a guardian against his will.

The Hindu Minority and Guardianship Act, 1956.

Section 6:

Natural guardians of a Hindu minor:-

The natural guardians of a Hindu minor, in respect of the minor's person as well as in respect of the minor's property (excluding his or her undivided interest in joint family property), are-

(a) in the case of a boy or an unmarried girl—the father, and after him, the mother: provided that the custody of a minor who has not completed the age of five years shall ordinarily be with the mother;

(b) in the case of an illegitimate boy or an illegitimate unmarried girl—the mother, and after her, the father;

(c) in the case of a married girl—the husband;

Provided that no person shall be entitled to act as the natural guardian of a minor under the provisions of this section—

(a) if he has ceased to be a Hindu, or

(b) if he has completely and finally renounced the world by becoming a hermit (vanaprastha) or an ascetic (yati or sanyasi)

Explanation:- In this section, the expressions 'father' and 'mother' do not include a step-father and a step-mother.

Section 13:

Welfare of minor to be paramount consideration:–

(1) In the appointment or declaration of any person as guardian of a Hindu minor by a court, the welfare of the minor shall be the paramount consideration.

(2) No person shall be entitled to the guardianship by virtue of the provisions of this Act or any law relating to guardianship in marriage among Hindus, if the Court is of opinion that his or her guardianship will not be for the welfare of the minor.

The Hindu Marriage Act, 1955

Section 26:

Custody of children:-

In any proceeding under this Act, the Court may, from time to time, pass such interim orders and make such provisions in the decree as it may deem just and proper with respect to the custody, maintenance, and education of minor children, consistently with their wishes, wherever possible, and may, after the decree, upon application by petition for the purpose, make from time to time, all such orders and provisions with respect to the custody, maintenance, and education of such children as might have been made by such decree or interim orders in case the proceedings for obtaining such decree were still pending, and the Court may also from time to time revoke, suspend, or vary any such orders and provisions previously made.

The Divorce Act, 1869

Section 41:

Power to make orders as to custody of children in suit for separation:–

In any suit for obtaining a judicial separation the Court may from time to time, before making its decree, make such interim orders, and may make such provision in the decree, as it deems proper with respect to the custody, maintenance and education of the minor children, the marriage of whose parents is the subject of such suit, and may, if it think fit, direct proceedings to be taken for placing such children under the protection of the said Court:

[Provided that the application with respect to the maintenance and education of the minor children pending the suit, shall, as far as possible, be disposed of within sixty days from the date of service of notice on the respondent.]

Section 43:

Power to make orders as to custody of children in suits for dissolution or nullity:–
In any suit for obtaining a dissolution of marriage or a decree of nullity of marriage instituted in a District Court, the Court may, from time-to-time before making its decree, make such interim orders as it may deem proper with respect to the custody, maintenance and education of the minor children, the marriage of whose parents is the subject of the suit,

and may, if it think fit, direct proceedings to be taken for placing such children under the protection of the Court.

Parsi Marriage and Divorce Act, 1936.

Section 49:

Custody of children–
In any suit under this Act, the Court may from time to time pass such interim orders and make such provisions in the final decree as it may deem just and proper with respect to the custody, maintenance and education of the children under the age of eighteen years, the marriage of whose parents is the subject of such suit, and may, after the final decree upon application, by petition for this purpose, make, revoke, suspend or vary from

time to time all such orders and provisions with respect to the custody, maintenance and education of such children as might have been made by such final decree or by interim orders in case the suit for obtaining such decree were still pending:

[Provided that the application with respect to the maintenance and education of such children during the suit, shall, as far as possible, be disposed of within sixty days from the date of service of notice on the respondent.]

Delhi High Court Rules
(Practice & Procedure)

Guardians and Wards

Part A GENERAL

1. Sub-Judges* empowered to try cases under the Act— Under Section 4A(1) of the Guardians and Wards Act, 1890, as amended by Act IV of 1926, the High Court may, by general or special order, empower any officer exercising original Civil Jurisdiction subordinate to a District Court, or authorise the Judge of any District Court to empower any such officer subordinate to him, to dispose of any proceedings under this Act transferred to such officer under the provisions of this section. The Hon'ble Judges have decided that with a few exceptions all the work under the Guardians and Wards Act should be entrusted to a Special 1 Class Sub-Judge in each district.

---

* After establishment of Family Courts in Delhi, cases pertaining to appointment of guardian for the person of minor are now dealt with by the Family Courts as per clause(g) of the Explanation to section 7(1) of The Family Courts Act, 1984; and the cases pertaining to appointment of guardian for the property of the minor are dealt with by the concerned District Judge.

2. Minors interest is the main consideration in appointing guardians—

In appointing guardians, Courts should work on the principle that the interest of the minor is the main consideration (Section 7). Very often it will be found that an application for the appointment of a guardian has been made in the interest not of the minor but of the applicant, especially when the application is for the guardianship of an unmarried girl.

3. Discretion of Court in appointing a guardian and issuing notices of application—

It does not follow that because an application is made for the appointment of a guardian, one must necessarily be appointed. Every application for guardianship should be laid at once before the Judge, who should only issue notice if he is satisfied after examination of the applicant (except when the applicant is the Collector) that there is ground for proceedings on the application under Section 11 of the Act, and even then, he should exercise a careful discretion as the persons to whom notice should be issued [Section 11(1)(a)(iv)]. It should also be noted that in certain cases a guardian cannot be appointed under the Act (Section 19). In appointing a guardian the Court shall be guided by the provisions of Section 17.

4. Reasons for rejecting an application in *limine* should be recorded—

If any application is rejected in *limine* the Court must give its reasons for rejection as an appeal lies under Section 47(a) of the Act.

5. No need to appoint a guardian of a deceased military servant for purposes of pension—

Court should not appoint a guardian, under the Guardians and Wards Act, merely in order to enable the heir of a man who has died in military service to draw a pension. A certificate signed by a Revenue Officer of or above the rank of a Naib-Tahsildar is accepted as sufficient authority for the payment of such pensions to *de facto* guardians.

6. Petty cases, proceedings should terminate appointment of guardian—

By Rule 8 of the rules framed under the Guardians and Wards Act, 1890, accounts are required (*vide* Part B of this Chapter) from guardians only when the annual income of the estate is likely to exceed Rs. 500 and in other cases only if the Court thinks fit to order. Having regard to the petty sums involved in the vast majority of cases, it should be the rule and not the exception that the latter class of proceeding should terminate with the appointment of the guardian. Continuous control is desirable only in the case of large properties.

7. Forms of Bank account for current expenses—

Attention is drawn to Rule 13 of the rules framed under the Guardians and Wards Act, 1890 (*vide* Part B of this Chapter). With respect to money required for the current expenses of the estate and of the ward's maintenance, which is not to be invested, that rule lays down no restriction as to the form of account, ie. current account, saving account, or fixed deposit account in which it may be placed. Such money should be placed in such form of Bank account as will be to the best interest of the minor.

8. Restrictions regarding withdrawal from Bank account—
When permitting the opening of an account in a Bank, the Court may direct that no withdrawal should be made by the guardian from the account except under the orders of the Court. If such restrictions are imposed on the powers of a guardian, they should be embodied in the guardianship certificate; or if a separate order to this effect is recorded, an attested copy of it should be forwarded to the Bank for registration along with an attested copy of the guardianship certificate. The Court should see in particular that the amounts kept in the Bank are no larger than are sufficient for current expenses and that all surplus money is invested in accordance with Rule 13 of the rules framed under the Guardians and Wards Act, 1890, (*vide* Part B of this Chapter).

9. Cases in which money for current expenses are to be deposited in treasury—
In case falling under Rule 14, money required for current expenses must be deposited in the treasury and the surplus money invested in Government Promissory Notes as laid down therein.

10. Pass books etc. to be kept by guardian—
All pass books, Government Promissory Notes, and Post Office Cash Certificates relating to Accounts of minors should be kept by their guardians and inspected by the Court at least once a year.

257th Report of Law Commission of India (Summary of Recommendations)

6.1 The recommendations of the Law Commission in this report are captured in the Hindu Minority and Guardianship (Amendment) Bill, 2015, and the Guardians and Wards (Amendment) Bill, 2015, which are appended to the report. The Bills, respectively, amend the Hindu Minority and Guardianship Act, 1956, and the Guardians and Wards Act, 1890. In this regard, the Law Commission also makes incidental reference to some of the recommendations of the 83rd report (1980) of the Law Commission, entitled 'The Guardians and Wards Act, 1890 and certain provisions of the Hindu Minority and Guardianship Act, 1956,'[37] as well as the 133rd report (1989) of the Law Commission, entitled 'Removal of discrimination against women in matters relating to guardianship and custody of minor children and elaboration

37 Law Commission of India, 83rd Report, April (1980); available at http://lawcommissionofindia.nic/51-100/Report83.pdf

of the welfare principles.[38]

6.2 The Commission provides detailed legislative text by recommending the insertion of a new chapter IIA dealing with 'Custody, Child Support and Visitation Arrangements'. The Commission also provides specific guidelines to assist the court in deciding such matters, including processes to determine whether the welfare of the child is met; procedures to be followed during mediation; and factors to be taken into consideration when determining grants for joint custody. The recommendations are discussed in detail in the following pages.

A. Amendments to the Hindu Minority and Guardians Act, 1956

6.3 The Law Commission recommends the following amendments to this Act:

1. Section 6(a): This section lists the natural guardians of a Hindu minor, in respect of the minor's person and property (excluding his or her undivided interest in joint family property). In the case of a boy or an unmarried girl, this section clearly states that the natural guardian of a Hindu minor is the father, and after him the mother. Even after the Supreme Court's judgment in Gita Hariharan v Reserve Bank of India,[39] the mother can become a natural guardian during the lifetime of the father only in exceptional circumstances. This is required to be changed to fulfil the principles of equality enshrined in Article 14 of the Constitution.

38 Law Commission of India, 133rd Report, August (1989); available at http://lawcommissionofindia.nic/101-169/Report133.pdf

39 (1999) 2 SCC 228

Accordingly, the Law Commission recommends that this superiority of one parent over the other should be removed, and that both the mother and the father should be regarded, simultaneously, as the natural guardians of a minor. This also follows from the recommendation of the Commission that the welfare of the minor must be the paramount consideration in every circumstance. This concept of welfare being paramount is already captured in Section 13 of the 1956 Act. In recommending such an amendment to Section 6, the Commission reaffirms the recommendations of its 133rd report, to give equal rights to both the mother and father in respect of a minor and his/her property.[40] It also reaffirms the recommendations of the 83rd report of the Law Commission, in intending the two provisions (Sections 6 and 13) to be read together.[41] Such a reading will necessarily imply that neither the father nor the mother of a minor can, as of a right, claim to be appointed by the court as the guardian unless such an appointment is for the welfare of the minor.

The Guardians and Wards Act, 1890 has also undergone similar legislative changes, moving away from an absolute and natural right of a father to be the guardian.[42] The 1890 law was enacted at a time when women had limited rights in law, and it was in need of reform. According to the older version of Section 19(b) of the 1890 Act, the court could not appoint

---

40 Law Commission of India, 133rd Report, August (1989); available at http://lawcommissionofindia.nic/101-169/Report1383.pdf]

41 Law Commission of India, 83rd Report, April (1980); available at http://lawcommissionofindia.nic/51-100/Report.83.pdf])

42 Venkata Narasiah Vs Peddiraja 1970 (1) ALT 25; Kumarswami Mudaliar Vs Rajammal AIR 1957 Mad. 563

a guardian of a minor (other than a married female), if the minor's father was living and not unfit to be the guardian. The Personal Laws (Amendment) Act, 2010 amended this clause to refer also to the mother in the same vein as the father, thereby making the law more equitable.[43] The recommendations of the Commission, in context of the changes to the 1890 Act, therefore, are merely removing anomalies in one law that have already been removed in another.

The proviso to section 6(a) presently provides that the custody of a minor below 5 years of age will ordinarily be with the mother. The Commission believes that this position should be allowed flexibility in cases where the court decides to grant joint custody, and the text of the provision is amended accordingly.

2. Section 7: This section provides that the natural guardianship of an adopted son who is a minor passes, on adoption, to the adoptive father and after him to the adoptive mother. The language of this section is incongruous in that it refers only to the natural guardianship of an adopted son, and does not refer to an adopted daughter. The Hindu Minority and Guardianship Act, 1956 came into force at a time when the general Hindu law as administered by the courts did not recognise the adoption of a daughter. Thus, at the time of passing of the Act, the adoption of daughters was only allowed under custom and not under codified law. This explains the reason why the drafters of the Act included the guardianship of

43 Personal Laws (Amendment) Act, No. 30 of 2010, Chapter-II

only adopted sons and ignored the adoption of daughters.[44] It was also enacted before the Hindu Adoptions and Maintenance Act, 1956, which corrected the legal position of adoption of a daughter statutorily.[45] The effect of the later law is that the adoptive father and the adoptive mother would be regarded as the natural guardians of the adopted child.[46] It follows that the Hindu Minority and Guardianship Act, 1956 should also include both an adopted son and an adopted daughter within the scope of natural guardianship. The Commission merely corrects this by amending the Hindu Minority and Guardianship Act, 1956 to be in consonance with the Hindu Adoptions and Maintenance Act, 1956. Further, the Commission recommends that the natural guardians of an adopted child should include both the adoptive parents, in keeping with its recommendations to Section 6(a) provided above, and previous legislative changes such as the Personal Laws (Amendment) Act, 2010. Accordingly, the Commission recommends that Section 7 be amended to refer to the natural guardianship of an adopted child who is a minor, which will pass, upon adoption, to the adoptive mother and father.

B. Amendments to the Guardians and Wards Act, 1890

6.4 The Law Commission recommends the following amendments to this Act:

1. Section 17: This section provides for matters to be considered by the court in appointing the guardian of a minor, and

---

44 Paras Diwan, LAW OF ADOPTION, MINORITY, GUARDIANSHIP & CUSTODY, 3rd edn. 2000, p. 226

45 Hindu Adoption & Maintenance Act, No. 78 of 1956

46 MULLA HINDU LAW, ed. Satyajeet A. Desai, 21st edn. 2010. p. 1258.70

requires the welfare of a minor to be consistent with the laws to which the minor is subject. In the past, Section 17 was read with Section 19 of this Act (which deals with the preferential right of natural guardianship).[47] Before being amended by the Personal Laws (Amendment) Act, 2010, Section 19 offered a preferential right to the husband (of a minor girl), or the father (in all other cases) to be the guardian of the minor, if neither were unfit to be appointed guardian. The 2010 Act included the mother along with the father as a natural guardian of the child, and changed the position of the law slightly.[48] However, the welfare of the child was still not, under law, truly the paramount consideration in such matters.

The Law Commission recommends that the possibility of any alternate reading be corrected in statute, and reaffirms, in this context, the general recommendations made by the 83rd report of the Law Commission. Thus, in the appointment or declaration of a guardian, the welfare of the minor must be paramount, and everything else must be secondary to this consideration. In determining welfare, however, the court may give due regard to the laws to which the minor may be subject. As the 83rd report observed, 'such an amendment will settle the position for all times to come,'[49] and will remove the possibility of the appointment of a guardian without first assessing welfare.

2. Section 19: This section provides for the preferential right of certain persons to be regarded as natural guardians. It provides

---

47 Law Commission of India, 83rd Report, April (1980); available at http://lawcommissionofindia.nic/51-100/Report.83.pdf

48 Personal Laws (Amendment) Act No. 30 of 2010, Chapter-II

49 Law Commission of India, 83rd Report, April (1980); available at http://lawcommissionofindia.nic/51-100/Report.83.pdf

that the court may not appoint a guardian, if the husband of a minor who is a married female is not unfit to be the guardian of her person, or if the father or mother (who are living) of a minor other than a married female is similarly not unfit to be the guardian. Here, too, the Commission reaffirms the 83rd report regarding the importance of the welfare principle, and recommends that in determining whether a person is unfit to be a guardian in these circumstances, the welfare of the minor under Section 17 shall be the paramount consideration.

3. Section 25: This section provides for the arrest of a ward if the ward leaves or is removed from the custody of his guardian, if such arrest is for the welfare of the ward. As with its recommendations above, the Law Commission concurs with its 83rd report, in various aspects. First, the concept of arrest of a minor is an archaic one, and needs to be amended to reflect modern social considerations. Therefore, the Law Commission recommends a substitute section, replacing 'arrest' with the requirement to return the ward to the custody of his or her guardian. Again, the Commission reiterates the necessity of placing the welfare of the minor as the paramount consideration.

Second, the present text of the law is unclear as to whether a guardian who has never had custody of a minor is entitled to the relief under this section. This needs to be clarified, and accordingly, the Law Commission reiterates the recommendations of the 83rd report as regards the language of the provision to specifically state that it applies in cases where the child is not in the custody of the guardian, though the latter is entitled to such custody.

Third, it recommends that the court must not make an order under this section in respect of a child of over fourteen years of age, without taking into consideration the wishes of the child. This is in consonance with the provisions of Section 17 of this Act, which allows the court to consider the stated preference of a minor, if the minor is old enough to form an intelligent preference. In a scenario where the minor of over fourteen years of age has left or been removed from the custody of his or her guardian, the Commission recommends that the court must take into consideration the preference of the child.

4. **Insertion of new Chapter IIA:** This chapter deals with custody, child support and visitation issues, covering a range of topics as discussed below.

a. Section 19A: Objectives of the chapter.

This section lays down the principal objectives of this chapter, by way of guidance to the court as to what the chapter seeks to achieve. Children are the most vulnerable persons in a matrimonial dispute, and the trauma that they face during and after the legal determination of such disputes is immeasurably harsh. Children often become pawns in such matters, and are used by their parents for their own purposes, to strike bargains that rarely take into consideration the emotional, social and mental upheavals that the children themselves may be facing. The Commission believes this imbalanced situation can be addressed in some measure through legislative changes that will place a duty upon the court to uphold the child's welfare in each and every circumstance, regardless of the individual interests of the parties involved.

These objectives, therefore, embody the fundamental and

most important recommendation of the Law Commission, regarding the welfare of the child being of utmost consideration. A court is bound to bear in mind these objectives in making an order under this chapter, and will therefore be required to comprehensively assess the consequences of any order it makes in light of these objectives.

The objectives require that the welfare of a child is met by ensuring various other aspects, such as recognising the changing emotional, intellectual, and physical needs of the child; maintaining a healthy and continuing relationship with both parents, society and siblings; recognising the prior and future ability and commitment of the parents to participate in the growth of the child; protecting the child from violence of any kind, and so on.

b. Section 19B: Applicability of this chapter

Custody issues are dealt with in three personal laws, which are, the Indian Divorce Act, 1869 (Sections 41 and 43), the Parsi Marriage and Divorce Act, 1936 (Section 49), and the Hindu Marriage Act, 1955 (Section 26). In general terms, these sections grant the court the power to pass decree/order regarding the custody, maintenance and education of minor children, whose parents are parties to a suit for divorce or separation.

The new chapter IIA as recommended by the Law Commission provides for detailed considerations in custody matters, and in that regard, is in addition to the powers of the court as listed in the three personal laws. This new section clarifies that the provisions of this new chapter will apply to all proceedings related to custody and child support, including under the three laws. This cross-reference to the personal laws is provided in the statute to clarify that the recommendations of the Commission are intended to be secular, and applicable to all persons, regardless of the personal laws they may be governed by.

c. Section 19C: Definitions.

This section offers two key definitions, ie., joint custody and sole custody. Joint custody is where both parents share physical custody of the child (in such proportion as the court determines to be for the welfare of the child), and also equally share the responsibility for the care and control of the child, and decision-making authority. Sole custody is a situation where one parent retains the physical care and control of a child. However, these rights may be subject to the power of the court to grant visitation rights to the other parent.

The introduction of joint custody as a defined term is to recognise the possibility, in law, of a court issuing an order of joint custody, if it is for the welfare of the child. However, the definition of joint custody, and the substantive provisions that follow, must always be read in light of the objectives that open the chapter, which seek to ensure that the custody arrangement eventually granted is always subject to the welfare of the child being met.

d. Section 19D: Award of custody.

This section gives powers to the court to make different kinds of custody orders. However, it also requires the court to consider the detailed guidelines contained in the schedule in this regard. The court retains the power to modify the orders so made, provided such modifications remain in the welfare of the child, and the reasons for such modification are recorded.

e. Section 19E: Power to pass additional orders.

This is an additional power granted to the court, necessary to effectuate or enforce any order relating to the custody of the child under the chapter.

f. Section 19F: Mediation.

Many disputes arising out of divorce proceedings (child custody, child support, etc.) could be solved through mediation. This would promote better outcomes for both parents and children, as well as reduce the strain on the overburdened court system. Before engaging directly with the court system, the Commission recommends that parties to a custody matter must ordinarily consider mediation before the proceedings actually begin, or when the court so orders. The court will usually refer the parents to the court-annexed mediation centre. However, in case there is no such centre, the court may appoint an individual mediator.

At present, Family Courts take assistance from marriage counsellors in settling disputes. Counsellors are different from mediators in terms of their approach. Counselling usually requires identifying behavioural issues of the individual parties and tends to involve professionals trained in areas of mental health, psychology, and sociology, unlike mediation, which requires identifying conflict behaviour and tends to involve professionals trained in dispute resolution.[50] Therefore, the Commission recommends that parties should be given the opportunity to participate in mediation with a trained mediator. Mediators

50 Marital Mediation Staff, What is the difference between Marital Mediation and Martial Counselling? February 22, 2013 available at http.// maritalmediation.com/ faqs/what-is-the-difference-between-marital-mediation-and-marital-counselling--.2/ (last visited on April 22, 2015)

should have appropriate background and training, including in family disputes. Further, High Courts, District Courts, and Family Courts should maintain a list of court- annexed mediation centres and individual mediators. These will be identified and paid remuneration in accordance with a scheme designed by the concerned High Court in consultation with the respective state governments.

As the legislation repeatedly emphasises, it is the duty of the court to ensure that the final custody order is for the welfare of the child. For this purpose, the Commission recommends that the court should have the power to obtain an independent psychological evaluation of the child, in order to determine various related issues (eg the child's preference, influence of and relationships with the parents, etc.). Further, as in the case of mediation, professional assistance may be required, as neither the court nor mediators may be qualified to understand child psychology.

Time-bound resolution is also a key factor to achieve the ultimate objective of ensuring that the welfare of the child is met. The Supreme Court has recognized that Family Courts should ensure that a reasonable time limit is prescribed for the completion of the entire mediation process so as to not delay the resolution of family disputes any further.[51] The Commission recommends that any mediation under this section must be time-bound, and must conclude within sixty days of being so ordered. In the absence of such a requirement, there is a risk that mediation may continue indefinitely and adversely affect the child in question. However, the court can extend this period, where necessary.

---

51 Baljinder Kaur Vs Hardeep Singh AIR 1998 SC 764

g. Section 19G: Child support.

Personal laws in India deal with the concept and idea of child support to some extent through the concept of custody of children in codified Hindu Law[52] and Parsi Law,[53] and the Indian Divorce Act.[54] However, these provisions do not list the reasons for which such child support is required. The Hindu Adoptions and Maintenance Act, 1956[55] has a provision for maintenance of children, but merely casts an obligation of maintenance on the father[56] as well as the mother.[57] Maintenance here means the provision for food, clothing, residence, education and medical attendance and treatment.[58] This definition of maintenance is generally worded so as to be applicable to all persons entitled to claim maintenance under the various provisions of the 1956 Act.[59] The Law Commission believes that child support in custody matters entails much more than the concept of maintenance as captured by the 1956 Act. Accordingly, it empowers the court to specifically pass orders for the maintenance of children. It elaborates that such an order will involve fixing an amount that is 'reasonable or necessary' to meet the living expenses of the child, including food, clothing, shelter, health care, and education.

However, terms such as 'reasonable' and 'necessary' may be construed as vague, and can be abused or wrongly interpreted

---

52 Hindu Marriage Act, No. 25 of 1995
53 Parsi Marriage and Divorce Act, No. 4 of 1869
54 Indian Divorce Act, No. 4 of 1869
55 Hindu Adoption & Maintenance Act, No. 78 of 1956
56 Krishnakumari Vs Varalakshmi AIR 1976 AP 365
57 MULLA HINDU LAW, ed. Satyajeet Desai, 21st edn. 2010
58 Hindu Adoptions & Maintenance Act, No. 78 of 1956
59 MULLA HINDU LAW, ed. Satyajeet Desai, 21st edn. 2010

when fixing amounts for child support. The Commission, therefore, qualifies these terms by recommending certain factors that courts must keep in mind when calculating child support. These include the financial resources of the parents, the standard of living of the child,[60] the physical and emotional condition of the child, his or her educational and healthcare needs or any other factor that the court deems fit for the child's welfare.

Following the general principle of majority being attained at the age of 18, the Commission recommends that child support must continue till such age of majority. There are cases where the court has advised an increase in the age of maintenance from eighteen to twenty-one and asked the Commission for its advice.[61] The Commission is of the view that the court should have the power to continue child support even after a child attains the age of 18, and wherever appropriate, this period may extend till the child reaches the age of 25, and not thereafter.

The Commission also recognises special treatment for children with mental or physical disability.[62] The Hindu Adoption and Maintenance Act, 1956, applies to persons with disability, but the benefits cease at the age of eighteen. The Commission recommends correcting the provision of law to provide child support beyond such time as the child reaches 25 years of age, in case of a child with mental or physical disability. The Commission recommends that courts should have the

60 Sayali Pathak Vs. Vasant Pathak 110 (2004) DLT 637

61 The Times of India, Raise Age for Child Maintenance to 21: Court, August 12 (2011), available at http:// timesofindia.indiatimescom/city/delhi/raise-age-for-child-maintenance-to-21-court/articleshow/9573821.cms (last visited on April 23, 2015

62 Juvenile Justice (Care and Protection) Act, No. 56 of 2000

power to order for the liability of the estate of a parent who dies during or after an order for child support is passed, to ensure that the welfare of the child remains the key, even after the lifetime of the parent.

h. Schedule: Guidelines

The Commission also recommends various guidelines to accompany the main body of the law, in the Schedule to the Bill. The guidelines discuss the following issues: factors to be taken into consideration when granting joint custody, determining the preference of a child, access to a child's records, parenting plan, grand-parenting time, mediation, visitation, decision making, and relocation.

The report was signed by the following:

Justice AP Shah, Chairman
Justice SN Kapoor, Member
Professor (Dr) Mool Chand Sharma, Member
Justice Usha Mehra, Member
PK Malhotra, Ex-Officio Member
Dr Sanjay Singh, Ex-Officio Member
Dr G Narayana Raju, Member-Secretary
R Venkataramani, Member (Part Time)
Professor (Dr) Yogesh Tyagi Member (Part Time)

Hague Convention On The Civil Aspects Of International Child Abduction

(Concluded 25 October 1980)

The States signatory to the present Convention,[63] firmly convinced that the interests of children are of paramount importance in matters relating to their custody, desiring to protect children internationally from the harmful effects of their wrongful removal or retention and to establish procedures to ensure their prompt return to the State of their habitual residence, as well as to secure protection for rights of access, have resolved to conclude a Convention to this effect, and have agreed upon the following provisions:–

63 This Convention, including related materials, is accessible on the website of the Hague Conference on Private International Law (www.hcch.net), under "Conventions" or under the "Child Abduction Section". For the full history of the Convention, see Hague Conference on Private International Law, Actes et documents de la Quatorzième session (1980), Tome III, Child abduction (ISBN 90 12 03616 X, 481 pp.).

CHAPTER I – SCOPE OF THE CONVENTION

Article 1

The objects of the present Convention are –

a) to secure the prompt return of children wrongfully removed to or retained in any Contracting State; and

b) to ensure that rights of custody and of access under the law of one Contracting State are effectively respected in the other Contracting States.

Article 2

Contracting States shall take all appropriate measures to secure within their territories the implementation of the objects of the Convention. For this purpose they shall use the most expeditious procedures available.

Article 3

The removal or the retention of a child is to be considered wrongful where –

a) it is in breach of rights of custody attributed to a person, an institution, or any other body, either jointly or alone, under the law of the State in which the child was habitually resident immediately before the removal or retention; and

b) at the time of removal or retention those rights were actually exercised, either jointly or alone, or would have been so exercised but for the removal or retention.

The rights of custody mentioned in sub-paragraph a) above, may arise in particular by operation of law or by reason of a judicial or administrative decision, or by reason of an agreement having legal effect under the law of that State.

Article 4

The Convention shall apply to any child who was habitually resident in a Contracting State immediately before any breach of custody or access rights. The Convention shall cease to apply when the child attains the age of sixteen years.

Article 5

For the purposes of this Convention –

a) 'rights of custody' shall include rights relating to the care of the person of the child and, in particular, the right to determine the child's place of residence;
b) 'rights of access' shall include the right to take a child for a limited period of time to a place other than the child's habitual residence.

CHAPTER II – CENTRAL AUTHORITIES

Article 6

A Contracting State shall designate a Central Authority to discharge the duties which are imposed by the Convention upon such authorities. Federal States, States with more than one system of law, or States having autonomous territorial organisations shall be free to appoint more than one Central Authority and to specify the territorial extent of their powers. Where a State has appointed more than one Central Authority, it shall designate the Central Authority to which applications may be addressed for transmission to the appropriate Central Authority within that State.

Article 7

Central Authorities shall co-operate with each other and promote co-operation amongst the competent authorities in their respective States to secure the prompt return of children and to achieve the other objects of this Convention. In particular, either directly or through any intermediary, they shall take all appropriate measures –

a) to discover the whereabouts of a child who has been wrongfully removed or retained;
b) to prevent further harm to the child or prejudice to interested parties by taking or causing to be taken provisional measures;
c) to secure the voluntary return of the child or to bring about an amicable resolution of the issues;
d) to exchange, where desirable, information relating to the social background of the child;
e) to provide information of a general character as to the law of their State in connection with the application of the Convention;
f) to initiate or facilitate the institution of judicial or administrative proceedings with a view to obtaining the return of the child and, in a proper case, to make arrangements for organising or securing the effective exercise of rights of access;
g) where the circumstances so require, to provide or facilitate the provision of legal aid and advice, including the participation of legal counsel and advisers;
h) to provide such administrative arrangements as may be necessary and appropriate to secure the safe return of the child;

i) to keep each other informed with respect to the operation of this Convention and, as far as possible, to eliminate any obstacles to its application.

CHAPTER III – RETURN OF CHILDREN

Article 8

Any person, institution or other body claiming that a child has been removed or retained in breach of custody rights may apply either to the Central Authority of the child's habitual residence or to the Central Authority of any other Contracting State for assistance in securing the return of the child.

The application shall contain:–

(a) information concerning the identity of the applicant, of the child, and of the person alleged to have removed or retained the child;

(b) where available, the date of birth of the child;

(c) the grounds on which the applicant's claim for return of the child is based;

(d) all available information relating to the whereabouts of the child and the identity of the person with whom the child is presumed to be.

The application may be accompanied or supplemented by:–

(e) an authenticated copy of any relevant decision or agreement;

(f) a certificate or an affidavit emanating from a Central Authority, or other competent authority of the State of the child's habitual residence, or from a qualified person, concerning the relevant law of that State;

(g) any other relevant document.

Article 9

If the Central Authority which receives an application referred to in Article 8 has reason to believe that the child is in another Contracting State, it shall directly and without delay transmit the application to the Central Authority of that Contracting State and inform the requesting Central Authority, or the applicant, as the case may be.

Article 10

The Central Authority of the State where the child is shall take or cause to be taken all appropriate measures in order to obtain the voluntary return of the child.

Article 11

The judicial or administrative authorities of Contracting States shall act expeditiously in proceedings for the return of children. If the judicial or administrative authority concerned has not reached a decision within six weeks from the date of commencement of the proceedings, the applicant or the Central Authority of the requested State, on its own initiative or if asked by the Central Authority of the requesting State, shall have the right to request a statement of the reasons for the delay. If a reply is received by the Central Authority of the requested State, that Authority shall transmit the reply to the Central Authority of the requesting State, or to the applicant, as the case may be.

Article 12

Where a child has been wrongfully removed or retained in terms of Article 3 and, at the date of the commencement of the proceedings before the judicial or administrative authority of the Contracting State where the child is, a period of less than one year has elapsed from the date of the wrongful removal or retention, the authority concerned shall order the return of the child forthwith. The judicial or administrative authority, even where the proceedings have been commenced after the expiration of the period of one year referred to in the preceding paragraph, shall also order the return of the child, unless it is demonstrated that the child is now settled in its new environment. Where the judicial or administrative authority in the requested State has reason to believe that the child has been taken to another State, it may stay the proceedings or dismiss the application for the return of the child.

Article 13

Notwithstanding the provisions of the preceding Article, the judicial or administrative authority of the requested State is not bound to order the return of the child if the person, institution, or other body which opposes its return establishes that:–

(a) the person, institution, or other body having the care of the person of the child was not actually exercising the custody rights at the time of removal or retention, or had consented to or subsequently acquiesced in the removal or retention; or

(b) there is a grave risk that his or her return would expose the child to physical or psychological harm or otherwise place the child in an intolerable situation.

The judicial or administrative authority may also refuse to order the return of the child if it finds that the child objects to being returned and has attained an age and degree of maturity at which it is appropriate to take account of its views. In considering the circumstances referred to in this Article, the judicial and administrative authorities shall take into account the information relating to the social background of the child provided by the Central Authority or other competent authority of the child's habitual residence.

Article 14

In ascertaining whether there has been a wrongful removal or retention within the meaning of Article 3, the judicial or administrative authorities of the requested State may take notice directly of the law of, and of judicial or administrative decisions, formally recognised or not in the State of the habitual residence of the child, without recourse to the specific procedures for the proof of that law or for the recognition of foreign decisions which would otherwise be applicable.

Article 15

The judicial or administrative authorities of a Contracting State may, prior to the making of an order for the return of the child, request that the applicant obtain from the authorities of the State of the habitual residence of the child a decision or other determination that the removal or retention was wrongful within the meaning of Article 3 of the Convention, where such a decision or determination may be obtained in that State. The Central Authorities of the Contracting States shall so far as practicable assist applicants to obtain such a decision or determination.

Article 16

After receiving notice of a wrongful removal or retention of a child in the sense of Article 3, the judicial or administrative authorities of the Contracting State to which the child has been removed or in which it has been retained shall not decide on the merits of rights of custody until it has been determined that the child is not to be returned under this Convention or unless an application under this Convention is not lodged within a reasonable time following receipt of the notice.

Article 17

The sole fact that a decision relating to custody has been given in or is entitled to recognition in the requested State shall not be a ground for refusing to return a child under this Convention, but the judicial or administrative authorities of the requested State may take account of the reasons for that decision in applying this Convention.

Article 18

The provisions of this Chapter do not limit the power of a judicial or administrative authority to order the return of the child at any time.

Article 19

A decision under this Convention concerning the return of the child shall not be taken to be a determination on the merits of any custody issue.

Article 20

The return of the child under the provisions of Article 12 may be refused if this would not be permitted by the fundamental principles of the requested State relating to the protection of human rights and fundamental freedoms.

CHAPTER IV – RIGHTS OF ACCESS

Article 21

An application to make arrangements for organising or securing the effective exercise of rights of access may be presented to the Central Authorities of the Contracting States in the same way as an application for the return of a child. The Central Authorities are bound by the obligations of co-operation which are set forth in Article 7 to promote the peaceful enjoyment of access rights and the fulfilment of any conditions to which the exercise of those rights may be subject. The Central Authorities shall take steps to remove, as far as possible, all obstacles to the exercise of such rights. The Central Authorities, either directly or through intermediaries, may initiate or assist in the institution of proceedings with a view to organising or protecting these rights and securing respect for the conditions to which the exercise of these rights may be subject.

CHAPTER V – GENERAL PROVISIONS

Article 22

No security, bond or deposit, however described, shall be required to guarantee the payment of costs and expenses in the judicial or administrative proceedings falling within the scope of this Convention.

Article 23

No legalisation or similar formality may be required in the context of this Convention.

Article 24

Any application, communication, or other document sent to the Central Authority of the requested State shall be in the original language, and shall be accompanied by a translation into the official language or one of the official languages of the requested State or, where that is not feasible, a translation into French or English. However, a Contracting State may, by making a reservation in accordance with Article 42, object to the use of either French or English, but not both, in any application, communication or other document sent to its Central Authority.

Article 25

Nationals of the Contracting States and persons who are habitually resident within those States shall be entitled in matters concerned with the application of this Convention to legal aid and advice in any other Contracting State on the same conditions as if they themselves were nationals of and habitually resident in that State.

Article 26

Each Central Authority shall bear its own costs in applying this Convention. Central Authorities and other public services of Contracting States shall not impose any charges in relation to applications submitted under this Convention. In particular, they may not require any payment from the applicant towards the costs and expenses of the proceedings or, where applicable, those arising from the participation of legal counsel or advisers. However, they may require the payment of the expenses incurred or to be incurred in implementing the return of the child.

However, a Contracting State may, by making a reservation in accordance with Article 42, declare that it shall not be bound to assume any costs referred to in the preceding paragraph resulting from the participation of legal counsel or advisers or from court proceedings, except insofar as those costs may be covered by its system of legal aid and advice. Upon ordering the return of a child or issuing an order concerning rights of access under this Convention, the judicial or administrative authorities may, where appropriate, direct the person who removed or retained the child, or who prevented the exercise of rights of access, to pay necessary expenses incurred by or on behalf of the applicant, including travel expenses, any costs incurred or payments made for locating the child, the costs of legal representation of the applicant, and those of returning the child.

Article 27

When it is manifest that the requirements of this Convention are not fulfilled or that the application is otherwise not well founded, a Central Authority is not bound to accept the application. In that case, the Central Authority shall forthwith inform the applicant or the Central Authority through which the application was submitted, as the case may be, of its reasons.

Article 28

A Central Authority may require that the application be accompanied by a written authorisation empowering it to act on behalf of the applicant, or to designate a representative so to act.

Article 29

This Convention shall not preclude any person, institution, or body who claims that there has been a breach of custody or access rights within the meaning of Article 3 or 21 from applying directly to the judicial or administrative authorities of a Contracting State, whether or not under the provisions of this Convention.

Article 30

Any application submitted to the Central Authorities or directly to the judicial or administrative authorities of a Contracting State in accordance with the terms of this Convention, together with documents and any other information appended thereto or provided by a Central Authority, shall be admissible in the courts or administrative authorities of the Contracting States.

Article 31

In relation to a State which in matters of custody of children has two or more systems of law applicable in different territorial units – a) any reference to habitual residence in that State shall be construed as referring to habitual residence in a territorial unit of that State; b) any reference to the law of the State of habitual residence shall be construed as referring to the law of the territorial unit in that State where the child habitually resides.

Article 32

In relation to a State which in matters of custody of children has two or more systems of law applicable to different categories of persons, any reference to the law of that State shall be construed as referring to the legal system specified by the law of that State.

Article 33

A State within which different territorial units have their own rules of law in respect of custody of children shall not be bound to apply this Convention where a State with a unified system of law would not be bound to do so.

Article 34

This Convention shall take priority in matters within its scope over the *Convention of 5 October 1961 concerning the powers of authorities and the law applicable in respect of the protection of minors,* as between Parties to both Conventions. Otherwise the present Convention shall not restrict the application of an international instrument in force between the State of origin and the State addressed or other law of the State addressed for the purposes of obtaining the return of a child who has been wrongfully removed or retained or of organising access rights.

Article 35

This Convention shall apply as between Contracting States only to wrongful removals or retentions occurring after its entry into force in those States. Where a declaration has been made under Article 39 or 40, the reference in the preceding paragraph to a Contracting State shall be taken to refer to the territorial unit or units in relation to which this Convention applies.

Article 36

Nothing in this Convention shall prevent two or more Contracting States, in order to limit the restrictions to which the return of the child may be subject, from agreeing among themselves to derogate from any provisions of this Convention which may imply such a restriction.

CHAPTER VI – FINAL CLAUSES

Article 37

The Convention shall be open for signature by the States which were Members of the Hague Conference on Private International Law at the time of its Fourteenth Session. It shall be ratified, accepted, or approved and the instruments of ratification, acceptance, or approval shall be deposited with the Ministry of Foreign Affairs of the Kingdom of the Netherlands.

Article 38

Any other State may accede to the Convention. The instrument of accession shall be deposited with the Ministry of Foreign Affairs of the Kingdom of the Netherlands. The Convention shall enter into force for a State acceding to it on the first day of the third calendar month after the deposit of its instrument of accession.

The accession will have effect only as regards the relations between the acceding State and such Contracting States as will have declared their acceptance of the accession. Such a declaration will also have to be made by any Member State ratifying, accepting, or approving the Convention after an accession. Such declaration shall be deposited at the Ministry of Foreign Affairs of the Kingdom of the Netherlands; this Ministry shall forward, through diplomatic channels, a certified copy to each of the Contracting States. The Convention will enter into force as between the acceding State and the State that has declared its acceptance of the accession on the first day of the third calendar month after the deposit of the declaration of acceptance.

Article 39

Any State may, at the time of signature, ratification, acceptance, approval or accession, declare that the Convention shall extend to all the territories for the international relations of which it is responsible, or to one or more of them. Such a declaration shall take effect at the time the Convention enters into force for that State. Such declaration, as well as any subsequent extension, shall be notified to the Ministry of Foreign Affairs of the Kingdom of the Netherlands.

Article 40

If a Contracting State has two or more territorial units in which different systems of law are applicable in relation to matters dealt with in this Convention, it may at the time of signature, ratification, acceptance, approval or accession declare that this Convention shall extend to all its territorial units or only to one or more of them and may modify this declaration by submitting another declaration at any time. Any such declaration shall be notified to the Ministry of Foreign Affairs of the Kingdom of the Netherlands and shall state expressly the territorial units to which the Convention applies.

Article 41

Where a Contracting State has a system of government under which executive, judicial, and legislative powers are distributed between central and other authorities within that State, its signature or ratification, acceptance or approval of, or accession to this Convention, or its making of any declaration in terms of Article 40 shall carry no implication as to the internal distribution of powers within that State.

Article 42

Any State may, not later than the time of ratification, acceptance, approval or accession, or at the time of making a declaration in terms of Article 39 or 40, make one or both of the reservations provided for in Article 24 and Article 26, third paragraph. No other reservation shall be permitted. Any State may at any time withdraw a reservation it has made. The withdrawal shall be notified to the Ministry of Foreign Affairs of the Kingdom of the Netherlands. The reservation shall cease to have effect on the first day of the third calendar month after the notification referred to in the preceding paragraph.

Article 43

The Convention shall enter into force on the first day of the third calendar month after the deposit of the third instrument of ratification, acceptance, approval or accession referred to in Articles 37 and 38.

Thereafter the Convention shall enter into force –

(1) for each State ratifying, accepting, approving or acceding to it subsequently, on the first day of the third calendar month after the deposit of its instrument of ratification, acceptance, approval or accession;

(2) for any territory or territorial unit to which the Convention has been extended in conformity with Article 39 or 40, on the first day of the third calendar month after the notification referred to in that Article.

Article 44

The Convention shall remain in force for five years from the date of its entry into force in accordance with the first paragraph of Article 43 even for States which subsequently have ratified, accepted, approved it or acceded to it. If there has been no denunciation, it shall be renewed tacitly every five years. Any denunciation shall be notified to the Ministry of Foreign Affairs of the Kingdom of the Netherlands at least six months before the expiry of the five-year period. It may be limited to certain of the territories or territorial units to which the Convention applies. The denunciation shall have effect only as regards the State which has notified it. The Convention shall remain in force for the other Contracting States.

Article 45

The Ministry of Foreign Affairs of the Kingdom of the Netherlands shall notify the States Members of the Conference, and the States which have acceded in accordance with Article 38, of the following –

(1) the signatures and ratifications, acceptances and approvals referred to in Article 37;

(2) the accessions referred to in Article 38;

(3) the date on which the Convention enters into force in accordance with Article 43;

(4) the extensions referred to in Article 39;

(5) the declarations referred to in Articles 38 and 40;

(6) the reservations referred to in Article 24 and Article 26, third paragraph, and the withdrawals referred to in Article 42;

(7) the denunciations referred to in Article 44.

Epilogue

It took me quite long to bring this book to its fruition. For me, it was about getting it right. It is deeply fulfilling when your work takes the shape and body you want it to. Till then, it just keeps flowing in and out of different moulds. This work has emerged from the life lived with the stories I have shared, and from what impacted me. Its intent is not fault finding but presenting before all stakeholders, especially all those adults fighting bitter battles for custody, the trauma they may unknowingly be heaping on each other and on their children, in their zeal to win the case.

All the stories I have shared, threw up one conclusion; behind different kinds of custody litigation runs the common thread of a parent's feeling of entitlement and distrust of the other parent. The focus primarily is on one's own rights rather than on the child's welfare. It is not that parents do not wish well for their children. But unknowingly, through litigation, they often heap indignities on the children.

Case after case revealed that custody litigation generally is more an execution of vendetta by one spouse against the other spouse. Issues are raised about the other's way of bringing up the child by pointing out deficiencies in the child's school performance, personality traits, etc. simply in order to show the custodial parent down and demonstrate that she/he is not fit for the job. This reminds me of the words of Pallavi Aiyar, who authored the book, *Babies and Bylines: Parenting on the Move,* that every scream (of her child) was a personal rebuke to her mothering skills.

A parent's pointing out of the child's deficiencies is intended as an assault on the parenting skill of the custodial parent, while presenting oneself as more capable to bring up the child, in order to win the battle for custody. In the process the child's self-esteem too may be seriously damaged.

Some stories (read cases) shook me out of my being. They made me aware of a possibility of my being labelled unfit and incompetent in bringing up my children; or of being dragged to a court for scrutiny of my mothering skills. It only takes a deft lawyer to uncover all your deficiencies in parenting and critique a child's character and personality due to alleged mishandling by the custodial parent. I counted my blessings for not being subjected to such ignominy and ridicule. I also realised how fortunate I had been to have received the love and affection of both my parents. My children too have been lucky in that respect.

I think everyone needs a chance to feel worthwhile. A chance to be the person one is, and to feel wanted and accepted as one is, whether it is a child or a parent. There is a noticeable change in trend with respect to child custody and sharing of custody between spouses. Till about a decade ago, in divorce settlements, generally custody of the child was retained by the mother/wife without too much contest. But lately, fathers are insisting upon retaining the custody of the child. If not full custody, they demand at least a right to equally share custody and claim a right in parenting of the child; they also claim their right to be part of the decision making with respect to every aspect of the child's life viz. the child's education, medical treatment if required, activities the child pursues, and even travel. Now the term 'co-parenting' is often referred to, which was not so, earlier. The courts were always conscious of the fact that the child needs the care and affection not only of both parents but also of grand-parents and relatives from both the sides for all-round development, which is the whole idea behind co-parenting, but the term 'co-parenting' was not used.

'Co-parenting' is a buzz word these days. I believe, it presupposes a lot of maturity on the part of both the parents and the family members on both the sides. It also requires a particular level of education and understanding which would take some time to happen in India.

Until about a decade ago, divorce was a taboo in India. It is only recently that it has to some extent been accepted as a way out when the spouses are extremely unhappy in a relationship and are not able to live together. Litigation for divorce, unless by way of mutual consent, is fought like a full-fledged battle till the judicial system tires the spouses out and they surrender to their fate. In such a situation, firstly drawing and then implementing co-parenting schedules becomes a herculean task. Courts find it difficult to execute custody schedules even if they have been agreed to mutually.

It has been an experience of the Family Courts that generally such schedules, though very helpful in saving the courts' time in disposing of custody/visitation requests on each occasion, give rise to a lot of collateral litigation/contempt petitions whenever the schedule is not followed strictly. The non-custodial parents keep count of the hours and minutes by which the child was produced late or taken away early.

As far as the parents who belong to lower/uneducated/ less educated strata are concerned, explaining to them the importance of sharing child custody and drawing a co-parenting plan jointly is itself a task.

Charts reflecting weekends, holidays, festivals, important days in life like birthdays, and so on—with these days being equally divided between the parents—are filed under the banner of co-parenting. I feel such regimented schedules hardly leave any room for human emotions and changed circumstances and constrict the organic flow of life. Such schedules demand 'army operation' like precision. Life, I think, does not work that way.

In the face of these challenges, the Family Courts have been doing a delicate balancing act of providing sufficient access to non-custodial parents for the healthy development of the child.

I hope the real-life stories in this book (names and personal details have been changed to protect identities) will act as a guide to parents seeking custody, so that they avoid the mistakes made by others in similar situations. Parents must be more sensitive to the feelings of traumatised children who have already suffered the loss of a secure two-parent home. I hope lawyers and my fellow judges who deal with tricky cases will benefit from my experience of the family courts.

Finally, everything boils down to the welfare of the child. Parents must remember that the child comes first.

Related Readings/References

- Law Commission of India Report No. 257 (Reforms in Guardianship and Custody Laws in India).
- Law Commission of India Report No. 133.
- Law Commission of India Report No. 83.
- Protecting Children by Protecting Their Parents – Vienna Convention on Consular Relations.
- Child Access and Custody Guidelines by NGO Child Rights Foundation, Mumbai.
- Guidelines on Shared Parenting – Colorado Department of Labour and Employment, Colorado Foundation for Families and Children.
- United Nations Convention on the Rights of the Child – an international effort to promote basic needs of the children as a fundamental human right (India along with 193 countries has ratified it).
- Hague Convention on the Civil Aspects of International Child Abduction 25 October 1980 (India is not a signatory to the Convention).
- Dibs In Search of Self by Virginia M Axline.
- The Children Act by Ian McEwan.